Nurturing Today's Children

Cultivating the Family of Faith

Gaynell Cronin and
Jack Rathschmidt, O.F.M. Cap.

Liguori/Triumph
LIGUORI, MISSOURI

Published by Liguori/Triumph
An imprint of Liguori Publications
Liguori, Missouri
www.liguori.org
www.catholicbooksonline.com

Imprimi Potest:
Richard Thibodeau, C.Ss.R.
Provincial, Denver Province
The Redemptorists

Copyright 2002 by Gaynell Cronin and Jack Rathschmidt, O.F.M. Cap.

All rights reserved. No part of this publication may be reproduced, stored in a retrieval system, or transmitted in any form or by any means—electronic, mechanical, photocopy, recording, or any other—except for brief quotations in printed reviews, without the prior permission of the publisher.

Library of Congress Cataloging-in-Publication Data

Cronin, Gaynell Bordes.
    Nurturing today's children : cultivating the family of faith / Gaynell Cronin and Jack Rathschmidt.—1st ed.
       p. cm.
    ISBN 0-7648-0839-7 (pbk.)
    1. Parents—Prayer-books and devotions—English. 2. Catholic Church—Prayer-books and devotions—English. I. Rathschmidt, John J. II. Title.

BX2352 .C76 2002
248.8'45—dc21   2002016117

Scripture quotations are taken from the *New Revised Standard Version Bible* (Catholic Edition), copyright 1989 by the Division of Christian Education of the National Council of the Churches of Christ in the U.S.A. Used by permission. All rights reserved.

Printed in the United States of America
06 05 04 03 02   5 4 3 2 1
First edition

Contents
■ ■ ■

Acknowledgment vii
Introduction ix
Using This Book xiv

I. Cultivating the Garden Soil
  The Sandbox 3
  Leftovers 7
  Alone Together 12
  Companions in Change 17

II. Blessing the Garden
  A Laughing Place 25
  Flavoring Everything We Do and Are 30
  Down Time 35
  The Habit of Gratitude 41

III. Watering the Garden
  Dealing With Fear 49
  Divorce: Offering Healing When Everything Hurts 55
  Death: Saying Good-Bye 60
  Frozen Feelings 65

IV. Tending the Garden Patch
  Sprouting Seeds 73
  A Safe Place 77

　　　　Fishing 82
　　　　Diversity 87
V. *Growing Garden Plants*
　　　　Helping Children Manage Loss 93
　　　　Honesty About Our Failures 98
　　　　Learning Patience 103
　　　　Our Household Church 108

Acknowledgment

Books do not write themselves. Deep gratitude to all who encourage our work, especially our families, parishes, and college community. Special thanks to Jean Marie Hiesberger, the editor of *Faith Works*, who encouraged us to write a column on the spirituality of children and families, and her husband, Robert Heyer, who introduced us to Liguori Publications.

Introduction

■ ■ ■

God's spirit is alive and active in the simple events of our daily lives. With every breath and step we take, if only we pay attention, God shows us a path to take, a destination, and the people with whom to journey. This startling gospel truth, which forms the basis for this book, as well as our own faith life, is too much for most of us to bear.

For us, spirituality means nothing more, and nothing less, than being attentive and responsive to the spirit of God who, while never manipulative, is very demanding. Listen to God's spirit in the groaning of creation, in the song of a bird, in the roar of the sea; taste God's love in the kiss of a child and the juice of a summer peach; see God's spirit in the first light of morning and the last glint of evening; smell God's love in newly turned earth, and incense that rises like prayer; touch God's love in the embrace of a lover and the hand of an enemy seeking reconciliation.

God, very simply, is everywhere. We have only to trust God's urging to open ourselves to the wonder and awe all around us, in good times and bad, sickness and health, sadness and joy, until death claims us for life everlasting. That is why we begin with a simple story taken from our own experience: a story of growth and change, of challenge and hope, of death and life.

The Strawberry Patch

A few years ago, our family planted strawberries. Even as a young child, I wanted to have my own strawberry patch, but because I lived in the South, where the hot and steamy weather would not permit the growth of strawberries, my dream was never realized. Then, when I became a parent, circumstances changed, and my children stepped in. Choosing a location three feet higher than level ground, and convincing me that it would be easy to frame it with wooden logs, they began. Working together, cultivating the soil, turning it, mixing it with new soil, even fertilizing and mulching, their eagerness was contagious. Every family member happily participated in this project. Just that alone was an extraordinary event! The results of their project were a bonus. All their care and working together brought the reward of big, round, juicy, red strawberries!

Runners

Undoubtedly, many of you know how strawberry plants grow. Shoots stream out from the main plant. At the end of each runner, a new plant forms, even while it is still connected to the parent plant. Because the soil, sun, rain, location, and loving care given to them were a perfect combination for our strawberry plants, they grew rapidly. Soon, we discovered new plants in many different places. While most of these plants found their way along the same level ground, settling not far from the parent plant, some were a little unorthodox. One group of plants hung over the side of our wood box, floating in the air. Another group of plants moved into the daisy patch, while still others had somehow grown down and under our wooden frame, emerging on the outside in a bed of rocks, far from home, yet healthy and attached to the parent plant. We marveled at the fortitude each runner had shown, as well as the originality of its choices!

Strawberries Grow Like Families

One early morning, coffee cup in hand, I walked through the garden. Eyes, ears, and heart open to whatever the morning light would bring, I was startled as I looked at our strawberry patch. "How much this plant is like a family," I thought. Children and other family members settle in the most unlikely places. Sometimes, like the strawberry runner that stays close to its parent plant, our children cling to us, tugging at our pant legs, holding on tightly as we try to walk and participate in daily life. These children are simply not ready to venture out into the world on their own.

Other children, like those runners that stretched out and moved into the daisy patch, venture into the most unlikely places. While we warn them of the dangers there and repeat the warnings passed down from past generations: "Tell me with whom you go, and I'll tell you who you are," our children seem perfectly happy, just like those runners in with the daisies, surviving well in places, and with people that are so diverse and different from themselves.

I also marveled at the unpredictability of those runners which settled among the rocks, outside the wooden frame, after having traveled underground, out of sight for such a long time. How frightening it can be when we don't know where a family member is emotionally, or even physically. They seem to move away from us in incomprehensible ways. While we try to reach them, waiting and praying, there is no response. Then, one day, we rediscover them (or they discover us), settled and relatively happy in a new situation or emotional place in their life.

And, of course, there is always someone in our family, like the runner that is blowing in the breeze over the edge of the wooden frame, conspicuous, even outrageous, hanging there for the whole world to see. While we are tempted to deny that this person is a member of our family, reminding everyone that there's another family in the next town with the same name, we finally have to admit they do belong to us.

Vine and Branches Stay Connected

The message of the strawberry patch for families is clear: *remain attached*. Give and receive life. Even when confused, frustrated, lonely, disappointed, worried, fretting, not knowing where to turn, or what step to take next, fearful of whether to speak or remain silent, to offer advice, correct, or admonish: *remain connected*. We must walk our family faith journey together, even when we are unable to see the path.

And love. No matter what happens: *give and receive love*.

Perhaps, I thought, if strawberries had grown in the land of Jesus, instead of the vine and the branches: he would have used the metaphor of "The Strawberry Patch" to describe the Church! How appropriate is that same image for our families!

Household Church

In recent years, the Church has spoken very extensively about the "domestic" or "household" church. Paul VI writes:

> *The beautiful name Domestic Church means that there should be found in every Christian family the various aspects of the entire church. The family, like the church, ought to be a place where the gospel is transmitted and from which the gospel radiates. In a family, which is conscious of this witness and mission, all the members evangelize and are evangelized.*

And John Paul II, in a homily given in Australia, in 1986, tells us:

> *The family is the domestic church. The meaning of this traditional, Christian idea is that the home is the church in miniature. The Church is the sacrament of God's love. She is a communion of faith and love. She is a mother and a teacher. She is at the service of the whole human family as it goes forward toward its ultimate destiny. In the same way, the family is a community of life and love. It educates and leads its members to their full human maturity and it serves the*

good of all along the road of life. The family is the first and vital cell of society. In its own way, it is a living image and historical representation of the mystery of the church.

Catch Faith

This pastoral development is the theological foundation for our essays in this book. Every couple, challenged by the rite of baptism, must become the "first" and "best of teachers" for their children. While this appears to be simple, it is no easy task. Our children need to "catch faith" from us through everyday family life. Being together in faith, listening carefully to one another's sacred stories, celebrating in our homes, and finding ways to reach out for the needy are the steps every family is challenged to take along the path of faith development.

Like the strawberry patch, even though we are moving in many different directions at once, we remain connected to one another, offering strength, hope, and launching a challenge to every parent and each individual in every home and household. We are the Church at home, the first church, and for some, the only church that our children will ever know. Our children deserve our best effort. This book serves as a tool to help you offer your best to your family through searching for meaning in the everyday events of life, and reinforcing your commitment to live faith one day at a time, making it a priority in your homes, neighborhoods, parishes, and world.

Are you afraid to face this challenge? Fear not, for Jesus says, "I am with you always, to the end of the age" (Mt 28:20). Perhaps, these words from the Gospel according to Matthew say it best:

> Look at the birds of the air; they neither sow nor reap nor gather into barns, and yet your heavenly Father feeds them. Are you not of more value than they?...But if God so clothes the grass of the field, which is alive today and tomorrow is thrown into the oven, will he not much more clothe you— you of little faith? Therefore do not worry... (Mt 6:26–31).

Jesus is and will be our *way, truth,* and *life.*

Using This Book
■ ■ ■

For more than twenty years, we have been working together: thinking, praying, reflecting, worrying, reading, speaking, and writing. Throughout these years together, we have paid special attention to families in their everyday lives and have found holiness everywhere, in the simplest acts of kindness, as well as the most profound acts of worship. God's people never fail to astound us! Or perhaps, it would be better to say that God's action in people is never difficult to find.

Because we are in awe of the everyday people who live in our neighborhoods and parishes who search out the needy and respond to the desperate, we have chosen twenty real but simple anecdotes from our work together to present here. Even though we have combined some stories and shortened others, all the people we write about here are real. Each and every one of them makes us pause, pray, and honor the God who lives in them, and challenges them to gospel transformation.

The order we chose for each essay was determined by the theme of the book. Because each "Strawberry Patch" needs cultivating, blessing, watering, tending, and growing before you can enjoy the fruit it produces, we have divided our book into sections that reflect this growth cycle in the hope that, when you finish, you will delight more fully in the sweetness and wonder of the gift of faith.

Each section begins with an explanatory introduction (Focus), followed by reflective questions. Because of the unique style of this book, you can begin anywhere you like. Pause for a few moments before you begin. Ask God to open your heart and spirit to a transformation. Then read on until something, anything, stops you. Pay special attention to those thoughts that come to you which may appear to be distractions. The spirit of God is often found in the most unexpected places! Ask yourself how God is reaching out to touch you as you read, then stop until the need to continue to read again moves you.

The few lines of poetry presented at the beginning of each reflection are offered in an effort to capture, through image and metaphor, the heart of what follows. Likewise, the questions throughout the text, as well as the simple gestures of faith suggested at the end of each essay, sum up the themes of each reflection. You can celebrate these ritualistic gestures alone, or with others, especially members of your families. Even if you only have a few minutes to spare, read and anticipate that God will touch you. God is always standing by, waiting, anxious to startle you with his love. Sometimes, God appears like a single rose or leaf, yet at other times, he appears as a laughing child, or a wise senior citizen. As Jesus reminds us, we have only to ask God to be with us, and he will hear and answer.

Faith is a wondrous gift designed to be experienced and celebrated. Let it wash over you like a cool summer stream, or strengthen you like a good night's sleep. God will be our guide, our peace, and our advocate. Like a defense attorney, God will always stand by us challenging us to be quiet, confident, and unafraid. We have only to enter into the life of Jesus to have everlasting life and have it to the fullest degree. Holiness is not something we earn, but the purest of gifts from God, the one who loves us totally, and unconditionally. We have only to accept this gift, live it, celebrate it, and give it away to others just as freely as God gives it to us.

I
Cultivating the Garden Soil
■■■

"I saw a gardener digging, turning over the soil, watering the plants at the proper time, persevering in this work."
JULIAN OF NORWICH

Focus

Both farmers and gardeners know how important it is to cultivate and prepare the soil if they hope to have a rich harvest. Jesus often used farming metaphors and parables to suggest that same idea. The parable of the sower is found in all three synoptic Gospels (see Mt 13, Mk 4, and Lk 8). If the soil is rocky, thorny, or shallow, we learn it cannot bear much fruit.

Mark's Gospel also asks us to think of God's reign like a tiny mustard seed, which when planted in good soil, grows into the largest of shrubs. Mark asks, "With what can we compare the kingdom of God....It is like a mustard seed, which, when sown upon the ground...becomes the greatest of all shrubs" (Mk 4:30–32). Likewise, if our strawberry patch is going to grow, we must prepare the soil.

In the following four essays, we must hoe, dig, and turn over the soil so that the roots of our faith can find a firm footing in which to grow. In the same way, we ask ourselves what must we do in our lives, families, neighborhoods, churches, and world in general to cultivate the soil so that, transformed by God's love, we can multiply a hundredfold so that the whole world might eat. Unless we are willing to spend time doing this first, and very arduous task, we will have little hope for the kind of juicy, ripe, red, strawberries the Lord wants to give us.

Reflections

As gardeners of our family garden patch:

- ■ How do we cultivate the soil of our home church?
- ■ What is the hard work involved in being a family?
- ■ How do we persevere in the struggles of everyday life?
- ■ How do we spend time in the garden of our family?

The Sandbox

As strong and secure
as my father's arms
when I was a child,
my pew holds me
in prayer.

Telling the Story

Sitting in the same pew where I sat for everything from private prayer to first communions, confirmations, and parish missions, I could not escape the bittersweet feelings of both loss and accomplishment. Thirteen years in the same parish as a director of religious education had flown by. Now, on my last day at Holy Name, I was sitting in my favorite pew again, this time to say good-bye. Images of delightful children, proud parents, worried catechists, and good friends were mixed with memories of my father's death, my niece's unsuccessful, but heroic battle with leukemia, and even my own serious illness. With very little effort, I found myself sitting in a pew that felt as secure as an ocean liner at sea, while praying in both gratitude and sadness.

That pew had always been a good place, a safe place, and a holy place for me. Every day that I worked at Holy Name I had stopped there for a few minutes just to center myself for the day, and prepare for whatever trials or joys it might bring. I wanted to be ready for the God who, so often, seemed to barge into my life when I least expected it. Frequently, when I felt overwhelmed by too many children to form in faith, and too few catechists to help, I slipped into my pew. And though I sometimes left too quickly, in a hurry to get on with the day, the visit to my pew never left me disappointed. My pew was a place where I met God repeatedly. Like Mary, Colin, and Dikon, who made their *Secret Garden* (Frances Burnett) into a gentle, healing place, only to leave it when they grew up, I would miss my pew immensely.

- Are you afraid of leaving a place, or work, or a home you love?
- How has God helped you during life's transitions?

Discovering the Meaning

Like Moses' mountain or my church pew, a sandbox can also be a place for reflection and change. I have watched my children and grandchildren quietly play in our sandbox for hours, creating both real and make-believe worlds. Listening to their simple conversations through the kitchen window, I eavesdropped on their happy times, alone and quiet times, as well as their sad and forgiving times after quarrels and upsets. And when I would call them in for supper, it's no wonder they would complain: "Oh, please, just a little longer." Who would want to leave such a wondrous place?

Sandboxes can be places of prayer. Like Jesus, our children need a definite time and place to pray. If we want them to handle fear, make gentle transitions, embrace both sadness and joy, and learn how to say both hello and good-bye, we need to provide them with prayerful places like a sandbox. And if not a sandbox, then as Shel Silverstein suggests, we can teach them about the places "where the sidewalk ends and before the street begins...."

- How can we create a "sandbox of safety" for our children?
- How can we help our children love quiet and silence?

Acting

Whenever we give workshops about the Church, we ask the participants whether anyone has ever asked them about how they decorate their homes. Usually, they look at us puzzled, and a little wary. Then, we remind them that their homes are "little churches" which deserve as much care be taken in their design as do our parish and world churches. Doesn't the story of "The Strawberry Patch" promise our children that they can always come home, no matter what happens?

Don't we ask them to find the courage to speak about their struggles and triumphs at home? In order to do this with more success, take a moment and ask yourself whether the design or layout of your home allows for a "pew" or "sandbox," where everyone, especially your children, can learn to pray? Homes that incorporate quiet places for reflection and prayer are much more likely to foster honest and stimulating conversation.

Remembering

On more than twenty instances in the gospels, we read that Jesus left the crowd behind and slipped away to spend time in prayer. The incredible pace of his ministry, the constant threats by the Jewish leaders, and his impending death drove him away from his friends to think, to have quiet time, and wait for God's direction and help. The seventeenth chapter in John's Gospel is stunning in this regard. Not only does Jesus pray to God for himself, he prays for his disciples and for us:

> After Jesus had spoken these words, he looked up to heaven and said, "I am not asking on behalf of the world, but on behalf of those whom you gave me, because they are yours....I ask not only on behalf of these, but also on behalf of those who will believe in me through their word, that they may all be one. As you, Father, are in me and I am in you, may they also be in us, so that the world may believe that you have sent me" (Jn 17:1, 9, 20–21).

While table prayer was an essential part of the Jewish life to which observant Jews gave themselves each day, the kind of prayer Jesus models in the gospels is different. The Lord moves away from family, crowds, and formality to be with his Father in quiet. By telling us about this aspect of Jesus' life, John reminds us that, despite the difficulty and darkness of Jesus' path, he cannot stop praying for himself, for his friends, and for all those will believe in him because of the work of his disciples.

Jesus' life of prayer and his commandment to his friends to "pray always" (Lk 18:1) reminds us that we need to do the same. No matter what happens in our life, no matter how confused, hurt, or lost we feel, like Jesus, we all need to find a mountain, a sandbox, or a "pew," where we can seek safety, insight, and solace.

- Do we model prayer for our children every day?
- Are we prepared to speak with our children about life's difficult paths?

Praying

God of All Quiet Places,
   Where is my place of intimacy and refuge with you? Is it a bench, a pew, a sandbox, a secret garden, a mountaintop? Where is my prayerful and holy place for quiet, silence, reflection—my sanctuary in time?
   We all need a place to remember what we love and who we are. Jesus had his place. Like him, let me leave the crowd and slip away to pray, think, to be quiet, and wait upon God. And do not let my prayer be self-absorbed, but let me remember all those who seek you in terrible darkness and want you to be a part of their daily lives.
   I so want to be one with you, loving God, and to walk with others in unity so that all will know you in us. So, God of All Quiet Places, like the child in a sandbox, hear my pleading voice, "Oh, please, just a little longer," in this wondrous place where you, Quiet God, always live. Amen.

Suggested Ritual

Create a definite time and place for prayer. Choose a space for a prayer table. Sit quietly, and imagine what belongs there. Allow images to arise: people, sacred objects, and things that hold a special meaning or for which you have a great love. Place and honor them on this table space. In quiet, rest there with God.

Leftovers

*Refrigerator boxes and old cardboard cartons,
like medieval churches,
hold mysteries aching to be discovered.*

Telling the Story

Sarah, Maggie, and Emma were delighted with their gifts. The leftover lace bows that had draped each bench in church for a wedding were a wonderful invitation to use their imagination in play. Shortly after supper, the three girls, aged eight, four, and three, like generations of children before them, invited their families into the backyard for a show. To Sarah's loud lead voice singing: "Taste and see, O taste and see, the goodness of the Lord," each little girl waved her lace wand and danced in circles. As their parents and adult friends watched, enraptured by the children's energy and endless joy, the children swirled around us, singing and dancing with abandonment. The more they danced, the more we smiled. The more they sang, the more we relaxed.

It had been a long weekend, full of too many duties and details, but the children's wonderful dance theater gently shook the tiredness from our spirits, and reminded us that God is never far away. How often children teach us, with only their imagination and playfulness to guide them, that life is about more than work, service, and discipline! Joy is the special gift they share with all those who are willing to "taste and see the goodness of the Lord."

Though some people may think that children receive too much attention and praise just for completing their everyday chores and assignments, young people, like Sarah and her cousins, need to hear us tell them how much their joy and wonder charm us and fill us with hope. Too often, we clap politely at their attempts to entertain us when, in truth, they have managed to change our outlook and lighten our mood in marvelous ways! How good it is to taste the joy they offer us as gifts of God's spirit!

Somehow, children know, even though we often fail to listen to them, that there is inherent value in the leftover objects our society discards. The ability to recognize and use leftovers creatively is a special skill of children. Who can't remember how exciting it was, as a child, to discover a refrigerator packing box? One could play in that box for days without getting the least bit bored!

- Take a moment, can you remember when a child touched your heart with joy?
- How can we keep wonder and awe alive in our own lives?

Discovering the Meaning

There is one type of kaleidoscope that breaks up and rearranges the patterns of objects we view, enabling us to look at something old in a new way. One rainy day, years ago, several neighborhood children came to our house to play—inside! What could we do? Then it hit me. I would let them use their "kaleidoscope eyes" in our string drawer. Scooping up the string, I placed it in a basket on the floor and watched.

Gwen decided to learn to braid. Barry knotted some string to pull his truck. Someone else made a picture on the floor, and Lydia crafted a necklace for her doll. Though fascinated, I had to stop them when they tied a piece of string to a kitchen chair for a jump-roping game of "'A' my name is Alice."

Adults can have kaleidoscope eyes too. Both myself and my children find it impossible to overlook an old, discarded piece of furniture that has been placed by the curb to be tossed out with the trash. We can't resist picking it up and trying to see what it would look like with just a "bit of work."

The poor in Calcutta also know the value of leftovers. A coconut is a great find: you can drink from its empty shell, or play it as a musical instrument, while the outer hairy rind can also be matted together to make mattresses. Notice that you will not find paper littering Calcutta's streets. Like birds gathering broken twigs for nests, its people use every leftover for some new purpose.

- Have we forgotten the gift of simplicity?
- How can we help our children enjoy and be satisfied with everyday things?

Acting

The process of creating is just as special as the creation itself. Each time we create, we learn something new. Our skills, talents, and gifts grow. Educators denote five levels of creating: *expressive, productive, inventive, innovative, and emergentive.* Full Christian maturity, reflective of the emergential level, is marked by our ability to change without losing our core beliefs and ideals, but children begin the journey at the expressive level. Therefore, offering children leftovers to play dress up, build a clubhouse, make an "our gang" wagon, or parade through the kitchen with utensils, singing their favorite song, is a wonderful way to help them develop their creative skills. It also enhances their progress towards Christian maturity.

The message seems obvious. We need not join the obsessive search for more and better products which our consumer-oriented society often implies is necessary for happiness. We have only to learn, like Jesus, to share a few loaves of bread, knowing there will be plenty of leftovers so that all people might eat.

Remembering

In Luke's Gospel we read the following:

> The day was drawing to a close, and the twelve came to him and said, "Send the crowd away, so that they may go into the surrounding villages and countryside, to lodge and get provisions; for we are here in a deserted place." But he said to them, "You give them something to eat." They said, "We have no more than five loaves and two fish—unless we are to go and buy food for all these people." For there were about five thousand men. And he said to his disciples, "Make them

sit down in groups of about fifty each." They did so and made them all sit down. And taking the five loaves and the two fish, he looked up to heaven, and blessed and broke them, and gave them to the disciples to set before the crowd. And all ate and were filled. What was left over was gathered up, twelve baskets of broken pieces (Lk 9:12–17).

Who doesn't love the story of the multiplication of the loaves? The sensitivity of Jesus to people's hunger, his insistence that his own disciples provide food for the hungry, and his graciousness in letting everyone eat as much as they liked all help us understand God's challenge for us to be as generous as he. After everyone eats their fill, there are still twelve baskets left over. In other words, there will always be enough "leftovers," if only we would gather and distribute them, to feed not only our families, parishes, and churches, but the entire world.

- Can you share an experience of using leftovers creatively?
- What faith lessons can you draw from these stories?

Praying

God of All Leftovers,
The everyday, the common, the ordinary, the discarded, the rejected—all of these hold mystery. When we use our imagination, a leftover comes alive in a new way. Give us kaleidoscope eyes, Creator God, eyes like yours, so we might imagine and rearrange new patterns and ways of seeing.

Let us dance and sing as we taste and see your goodness. For healing weary spirits and feeding hungry bodies, we fill our gathering baskets with leftovers, sharing and sustaining life for ourselves, our families, our world. Amen.

Suggested Ritual

Together, sing and dance to the Shaker folk song, "*Tis the gift to be simple*":

> 'Tis the gift to be simple,
> 'Tis the gift to be free,
> 'Tis the gift to come down
> where we ought to be,
> and when we find ourselves in the place just right,
> It will be in the valley of love and delight.
> When true simplicity is gained
> to bow and to bend we shall not be ashamed,
> to turn, turn, will be our delight
> 'Til by turning, turning, we come round right.

Alone Together

Somehow
I see so much better
In the dark
Where nothing matters
But love.

Telling the Story

Recently, one of my mother's closest friends died. A lively, funny, honest woman, she was legally blind for the past twenty years. She lived with many hallucinatory demons, sharing an apartment with her youngest son, Jackie. Now fifty and frail, Jackie appeared very anxious at the wake, unable to look directly at the people who came to offer their prayers and consolation. After having lived with his blind mother his entire life, his apartment was always dark. Largely because Jackie and his late mother had relied upon their sense of touch to feel their way around in the shadows, it appeared obvious that he was uncomfortable in the light. Even though he was surrounded by friends and family, he felt very much alone. His awkwardness and fear were evident to everyone, and we wondered how he would be able to continue on without his mother as his guide.

Kathleen Norris writes about people like Jackie in *Dakota*, her evocative "spiritual geography." Paraphrasing the poet, David Evans, she speaks of the Great Plains as a place where Native Americans and Anglos, because of centuries-old feuds and fears, "live alone together." Rereading *Dakota*, I thought about people like Jackie who live in families, rectories, and religious communities "alone together." And I thought of strawberry patches and our children.

Not infrequently, I hear children complain that they are bored. Like a slap in the face, the word itself stings, and I am often tempted to either rescue or correct them. Surrounded by books, toys, and people, unless they are stimulated from outside sources, they complain of having "nothing to do" and being "bored." Like Jackie, they are "alone together." They are people without either the ability or the imagination to entertain themselves and reach out to others. How I long for them to learn the value of quiet, prayer, and contemplation!

- Do you ever feel "alone together"?
- Are you happy and at peace this way?

Discovering the Meaning

Reluctantly, perhaps, most people recognize that the computer, like the radio and television before it, is here to stay. Wonderful at times, and almost magical, a computer can allow us to speak to people all over the world at the same cost as a local phone call or chat with other people who are also interested in Chinese cooking, hang gliding, chess, or whatever our favorite hobby may be. Wondering if Jackie had, or would like a computer, I quickly realized that computers can also be horribly isolating, and as compulsively addictive as alcohol. Jackie didn't need a computer. Like all of us, he needed a friend.

Before kindergarten age, children usually play alongside, rather than with, anyone who happens to come into the sandbox. Aware of the presence of others, but with no need to interact, they are healthy and happy being "alone together." But as they grow older, children's self-esteem arises from their ability to "fit in" and "belong." They accomplish this by developing the skills of *listening, communicating, cooperating, negotiating, sharing, and emphasizing.* Unfortunately, with today's family life so cluttered and frantic, the time and interaction necessary to develop these skills are hard to find. No wonder our children seem to emulate fantasy figures rather than real people!

- What can we do when our children seem to habitually isolate themselves from others by using music, television, or the computer as a barrier?

Acting

As parents, sometimes we need to structure situations so that our children may practice interpersonal skills. By remembering to be patient, and acknowledging both success and failure, we help our children develop the ability and capacity to experience community. Children who develop a social self are much more likely to understand and seek community life, as well as church involvement.

When Kathleen Norris was teaching a writing course, she worried about what to do about the very quiet Native Indian youngsters who were overshadowed by the presence of so many precociously verbal caucasian children. Remembering a time when she lived in a Benedictine community, she was inspired to create a "make silence" time for her children. Together in a circle, holding hands, she instructed everyone to remain quiet for at least one minute and look at one another. Despite the occasional jittery laugh, the children slowly began to smile at and listen to one another.

When we notice that certain family members are drifting into isolating pastimes and places, we need to make time for them to speak to us and tell their stories. Encouraging everyone to write down their feelings with respect to family difficulties gives introverted members more time to collect their thoughts and share their reflections. Though being a communicative family is hard work, it provides great rewards.

Remembering

In Luke's Gospel we read the following passage:

> "This fellow [Jesus] welcomes sinners and eats with them." So he told them this parable: "Which one of you, having a hundred sheep and losing one of them, does not leave the ninety-nine in the wilderness and go after the one that is lost until he finds it? When he has found it, he lays it on his shoulders and rejoices. And when he comes home, he calls together his friends and neighbors, saying to them, 'Rejoice with me, for I have found my sheep that was lost.' Just so, I tell you,

there will be more joy in heaven over one sinner who repents than over ninety-nine righteous persons who need no repentance" (Lk 15:2–7).

Jesus spoke about the lost sheep because the people in his era understood that sheep were naturally communal. They lived together in flocks. When one sheep was separated from the rest, it would frantically search for the others. However, if it could not find its flock, it would just lie down and stop eating and drinking. Unless someone found the sheep, it would eventually die.

When we sense that we or our children are lost, "living alone together," because of Sunday football or the incessant beeping of computer games, we need to recognize our isolation and let our friend, the Good Shepherd, find us again. When Jesus discovered his disciples, like lost sheep, "hiding in the upper room in fear" and isolation, he sought them out and said, "Peace, don't be afraid." He can do the same for us.

- Admitting we are lost is very difficult. How can we help our children admit their vulnerability?
- How can we convince them that there is a Good Shepherd searching for them?

Praying

Our Alone Together God,
An old song haunts: "I'm a lonely little petunia in an onion patch. Boo hoo. Boo hoo. Oh, won't somebody play with me?" Where are those somebodies? Have we isolated ourselves in so many onion patches that no one can find us? Sometimes we feel so lost, like the hundredth sheep. Vulnerability sweeps through us. Like your friends hiding in fear in the upper room, we, too, close and lock our door so no one can enter.

Faithful Protector, draw us away from isolation. Surround us and all the Jackies of our world with friends and family. Let us know we fit, we belong. Give us strength and help us develop skills so we can have a conversation with you and others. Amen.

Suggested Ritual

In silence, we sit in a circle of love around a burning candle. Become comfortable in the light and in the warm presence of one another: alone together as a family.

Companions in Change

*When the caterpillar
sheds her skin
is she testing her wings
or leaving forever?*

Telling the Story

Emma, a normally outgoing and self-revealing girl of ten, had become very secretive. Her mother asked if I had noticed anything different about Emma during our religious-education program. Her teacher told me that she had become quieter but was not disruptive in class, so I asked her mother to tell me a little about how she was feeling. "Emma has always told me everything," she said. "Almost as soon as she came home from school she would be chatting about her friends, her teachers, even what she did at recess. No more. I'm very concerned. She seems to have moved far away from me, and I don't know how to reach her."

Emma was the oldest child in her family, and her mother was experiencing distance from her daughter for the first time. Assuring Emma's mom that we would pay special attention to her daughter, I also encouraged her to give Emma some space and time to work through this awkward period in her life. While Emma's changes were probably normal and necessary, her mom had to come to terms with her own loss.

- How does it feel when a child begins to move away from you, like a new runner in a strawberry patch?
- How can you help a child feel "safe" when doing this?

Discovering the Meaning

Children change and when they do, it is difficult. While parents need to be attentive and responsive to any radical shifts in their children's behavior, they also need to respect the normal maturation process through which all children move, while also remembering that children need to find their own path and travel their own journey. Two simple rules (of the spirit) might help Emma's mother and us as well:

1. *We don't have to answer every question*, or know and understand everything about our children. Just last week, my granddaughter wanted to talk about how God could be both human and alive forever. Nothing I said made any sense to her. In her kindest voice, Sarah said: "Grandma, you don't understand what I mean."

   Listening to our conversation as he peeled potatoes, Sarah's dad had to turn away to keep from laughing out loud. Sarah was asking unanswerable questions. Though I was a bit unnerved, I wanted to protect her and say much more than a six-year-old could comprehend. I let go and told Sarah her questions were good ones and that understanding God is difficult. I also reminded her that parents and grandparents don't have answers to every question, but that I would always listen to hers and love her. Satisfied, Sarah said "thank you," and launched into a new area of conversation. By allowing our children to develop a locus of authority within themselves and honoring it, we powerfully demonstrate how much we respect them.

2. *We are not responsible for other people's choices*. Emma, for reasons that were not clear to anyone, needed to go inside herself. While her parents can gently ask whether she is all right, they don't have to pry, demand, or "fix" her. As parents, we don't always have to be in charge, directing others where to go and what to do. At ten, Emma is going to make choices of her own that might be uncomfortable for her parents and other adults. But she has a right to make these choices, as long as she does not seriously harm herself, or others.

While Emma's sudden secretiveness could be masking confusion and distress, it might also be a real compliment to her parents. Perhaps, beginning to find the voice that allows her to have her own opinions, she needs to test it within herself before speaking it aloud. Who, but her parents, prepared her to make this discovery?

- Have you ever read anything about a child's social and psychological development? What most impressed you about what you read?

- Who has been your most helpful companion during times of change?

Acting

At the summer solstice, the sun seems to be standing still. The days are long, and the nights short. Long ago, in festivals that honored the earth's awakening, people put thistles and herb wreaths in their homes as a means of protection against the dark. Families, trying to create a safe space where children and adults can explore difficult questions, might exchange thistles as a symbol of their commitment to walk with one another through every darkness.

Scheduling regular family time for sharing and conversation is another good way to assure everyone that we hear and respect the changes we all experience. A friend of mine has been very successful at stimulating family conversation by encouraging family members to write out, anonymously, on a slip of paper, any questions or concerns they might have, and put these slips into an empty vase that sits in the middle of their kitchen table. During family meals, one family member is asked to draw a slip of paper from the vase and read it aloud. Often, the question or concern is something that the family has already discussed, but without reaching any definite resolution. Allowing it to be anonymous fosters further discussion, without burdening any one person with the responsibility of having brought up something that may be uncomfortable and touch upon unresolved areas of family life. It also offers the family members a chance to look at and discuss the matter from a different perspective, perhaps after a "cooling off" period. This also sends the message that a certain unsettled matter needs further discussion and resolution.

Remembering

Luke's Gospel speaks directly about Jesus' growth, in both wisdom and age, and reminds us how difficult this was for his parents:

> Now every year his parents went to Jerusalem for the festival of the Passover.... When the festival was ended and they started to return, the boy Jesus stayed behind in Jerusalem, but his parents did not know it. Assuming that he was in the group of travelers, they went a day's journey. Then they started to look for him among their relatives and friends. When they did not find him, they returned to Jerusalem to search for him. After three days they found him in the temple, sitting among the teachers, listening to them and asking them questions. And all who heard him were amazed at his understanding and his answers. When his parents saw him they were astonished; and his mother said to him, "Child, why have you treated us like this? Look, your father and I have been searching for you in great anxiety" (Lk 2:41–48).

Because Jesus lived in a culture that permitted little variation from the norm, his act of "staying behind" in Jerusalem not only deeply confused his parents, it angered them. Mary's anxiety bursts out in her question to Jesus, blaming him for her upset. One wonders whether Jesus' explanation helps at all. Though Mary and Joseph do not seem to understand what their son was saying, perhaps they were consoled by remembering the difficult choices they had to make when Jesus was conceived and after he was born. If, as parents, we can remember all the stages of growth which we experienced, we might be much more accepting of the changes our children experience.

- Do we think to look to the Scriptures for help throughout our daily lives as parents?

- What are some healthy ways to help family members walk through periods of change in their lives?

Praying

God of Change,

Companion and gently ease us through change. We resist. Just when it seems that everything has finally come together, there is new movement and the seams of our lives are stretched. A chatty Emma becomes quiet, a questioning Sarah poses unanswerable questions, and we panic. Our strongest impulse is to pry, take charge, try to discover a reason, and direct others in what to do and where to go. We want to return to the way things once were.

Like Mary and Joseph anxiously looking for and finding Jesus in the Temple, let us return home and experience our loved ones growing in wisdom and age, according to who they are, and where *you* are, Gracious One, in their lives. Give us deep respect for the journey of others and the normal maturation process of life. Help us to see and rejoice in their finding their own voice, their own locus of authority.

Let us remember our own stages of growth. How quickly we forget that life is growth. And growth means change. Bless us, God of Change, through the different stages of our life. In the seasons of the earth—spring, summer, autumn, and winter—let us see, hear, and experience your companioning presence. You are yesterday, today, and tomorrow, the only constant in our life. Amen.

Suggested Ritual

Place four candles in a circle—one for each season of the earth. Light them. At this time in your life, name and bless where you are in the season of your heart. Bow out of respect for change and growth.

II
Blessing the Garden
■ ■ ■

"God will often come to take pleasure in the garden."
Teresa of Ávila

Focus

How often, especially in our postmodern, industrialized society, we take for granted the simple, yet essential, gifts of nature and grace! A stunning sunset stops most of us, but the slow growth of strawberries from seeds to flowers to fruit often escapes our notice. The miracle of growth, which can amaze and delight us if we would only pay attention, becomes a distant event, stripped of its powerful meaning.

The same can be true of God's action in our lives. The sudden awareness of an insistent, guiding presence startles us but, too frequently, we forget to be grateful. Watching a child gather flowers for her mother, or an older person helping a friend cross a heavily traveled street, lifts our spirits with hope and invites us to praise God for all things good and beautiful every day. Though we often fail to hear, the Scriptures remind us: "O taste and see that the Lord is good" (Ps 34:8).

The following four essays challenge us to take time today to be grateful for what we have, not for what we lack; to pause and wonder about how good God is and how helpful God has been; to weep and laugh with the Lord along the path to Jerusalem, that place of death transformed forever into life.

Reflections

In taking pleasure in our garden:

- ■ How do we practice gratitude?
- ■ When do we hear the sounds of play and laughter, engage in wonder and lighthearted fun?
- ■ How do we experience God's delight in us?

A Laughing Place

*Laughter, like music,
empties our souls
of needless concerns
and fills them
with joyful hope.*

Telling the Story

A number of years ago, when I was at a regional religious-education meeting, the priest who was leading us in a day of prayer very solemnly began, "OK everyone, let us bow our heads, screw up our faces and pray." When those of us, who were less constrained by the sober environment, peeked to see if he was really serious, we saw him smiling broadly, enjoying the fact that at least half of the people had not even heard him. He was poking a little fun at us very earnest folk who, though devoted to religious education, too often lose our sense of humor. As Reinhold Niebuhr says: "Humor is a prelude to faith, and laughter the beginning of a prayer."

In the *Song of the South,* Uncle Remus says, "everyone needs a laughing place," a dwelling where we face life's incongruities and where we are encouraged to express our amusement. Laughing places, like strawberry patches that are surviving, and even thriving in the most unlikely of places, help us to be amazed and surprised by the Spirit. In the story of the prophet Balaam, the donkey becomes a protector, in another story, a whale turns Jonah around for his mission, and in yet another, the very proper Zacchaeus climbs up and sits in a sycamore tree. Where is our own laughing place today?

We found one such place when we gathered with friends to celebrate the twenty-fifth wedding anniversary of a wonderful couple we know. As each gift was opened, the person bringing it was asked to share a memory they had of the anniversary couple. The stories began, and so did the laughter! The young people who were present listened, and watched with amazement, as the adults collapsed in laughter. Only the hostess was a little nonplused. "I did my best to initiate this ritual with the proper tone. Did I do something wrong?" "Nothing," we almost shouted, "we're having a wonderful time!" We needed a laughing place to welcome and renew our weary bodies and spirits.

One Sunday, my oldest granddaughter, Sarah, was laughing uncontrollably and her laughter became infectious. Her younger sister, Maggie, started laughing too. Soon, all of us were laughing and none of us, save Sarah, knew why. We just knew that our laughter felt good. Finally, Sarah's mother asked her why she was laughing so hard. Trying to catch her breath, Sarah finally blurted out a silly children's joke someone had told her in kindergarten. Even as she spoke, Sarah started laughing again, lost in her own world. Enjoying herself immensely, she was reminding us to enjoy the simple pleasures of everyday living. She knew what Meister Eckhart meant when he said that at the center of every experience is the laughter of God.

- Have you lost your sense of humor?
- Where did it go?
- What can you do to recover it?

Discovering the Meaning

Sarah's laughter made everyone, especially the adults present, stop for a moment. Too often, we find ourselves trapped in a very serious world. We worry about refugee children dying from starvation, obsess about what college our children should attend, and struggle with how to raise our children with faith in a world that is often overwhelmed with violence and greed. While the painful and depressing situations we are forced to address are real, so, too, is the goodness of all people of faith. Sarah's laughter reminded us to "lighten up," let go, and remember that Christians are called to be a people of joy, as well as justice. Otherwise, the natural gaiety and laughter of the child within us is lost and we would lose our ability to play. And as many notable psychiatrists tell us, play is an essential part of our lives.

An Apache Indian myth reminds us of this same truth. "The Creator made us to talk, run, look, and hear, but he was not satisfied until we could do just one thing more: *laugh*. And so men and women laughed, and laughed, and laughed. And the Creator said: Now you are fit to live."

- How can we bring joy and lightness to our families and parishes?
- Think gratefully of someone who brought laughter to you as a child. What did they do to make you laugh? Can you pass the laughter along?

Acting

Family gatherings without lightness or laughter will soon become occasions that everyone will find an excuse to avoid. If we discuss only the issues of the day, our gatherings will quickly become burdens that everyone feels forced to carry, rather than opportunities for renewal and refreshment. After all, didn't Jesus say: "Come to me all who are heavy burdened and I will refresh you"?

The dictionary defines a "sense of humor" as "the capacity to appreciate or understand," a definition that brings the heart into the matter. A compassionate and understanding heart is the core of laughter, grounded in a mature sense of humor that finds delight in the ordinariness of life, in the joy of what is. In *All Hallows's Eve*, T. S. Eliot speaks of "the laughter at the heart of things" which comes from the way we appreciate and understand life, with both its tragedies and joys.

Because we sometimes fail to notice the amusing events that regularly happen all around us, we asked some of our family members and friends to share a funny event they witnessed, or a humorous story about themselves. One young woman, now married with three children, couldn't wait to tell us about one such incident that happened in a shopping mall. Two very young children were trying to help each other eat a cup of chocolate ice cream. As she watched them struggle with the spoon and cup, she was drawn to remember birthdays in her own family when her younger siblings always had more ice cream on their faces and bibs than they did in their mouths! Her funny tale mushroomed into a delightful series of stories about our children when they were young. For more than an hour, we laughed and rejoiced in their memories of growing up together. As Garrison Keilor says, "Humor is not jokes and tricks, but a presence in the world that shines on everyone."

Once we get it going, telling delightful stories almost always leads to a feeling of profound peace in our family. Even when the stories told are painful, we still find ourselves listening more carefully to one another, finding new meaning for family life that, otherwise, might have escaped us. Fostering storytelling in our families not only helps us to let go of hurts, it also reminds us to be grateful for one another's goodness and accomplishments, and shows us how to become a presence in the world that shines on all people.

> *When voices of children are heard on the green*
> *And laughing is heard on the hill*
> *My heart is at rest within my breast*
> *And everything else is still. (William Blake)*

Maybe a hill could be our laughing place.

Remembering

In the book of Job, Yahweh, so full of pain and misery, reminds Job:

> "See, God will not reject a blameless person, / nor take the hand of evildoers. / He will yet fill your mouth with laughter, / and your lips with shouts of joy" (Job 8:20–21).

Sometimes, it is a good practice to read the Bible aloud and just let the words form pictures in our minds. Let your mind's eye see God literally pouring laughter into your mouth and touching your lips with joy. When Isaiah wanted to reject God's call to prophesy, he protested, saying that "he was a man of unclean lips." Undaunted, God sent an angel to touch his lips with a fire that would purify him of all his sins. We can also ask God for that same gift. Ask the Lord to touch your unclean lips and set your tongue free, not only to proclaim the Good News but to tell a simple, funny family story or joke. What a joy we can be for one another!

- What helps you laugh?
- What can help our families laugh and play more?

Praying

God of Laughter,

We are too serious, even in our prayer time with you. Invite us into your heart place where we can delight and laugh together about the incongruities of life. Your voice whispers: *Appreciate. Enjoy. Be amused. Be lighthearted. Have gaiety and joy.* Like Sarah, let us become lost in your world of delight, your laughing place of creation. The child in us yearns to laugh and play again, like the Wisdom figure of Scripture, "at your side, delighting, ever at play, at play everywhere in God's world."

Welcome all your people into laughing places, God, and renew our weary bodies and spirits. Places of delight are found in the ordinariness of everyday life. Grace us with that infectious "can't catch your breath" kind of laughter as we share the stories of our lives. With the mystic, Meister Eckhart, let us hear your laughter, God, at the center of every experience. Amen.

Suggested Ritual

Take a few moments to close your eyes and become aware of the way you are holding your mouth. Place a gentle smile there. Notice any change that comes to your feelings. At a family meal, invite family members to recall and tell a lighthearted story about themselves or a funny event they witnessed. Enjoy your laughing place together.

Flavoring Everything We Do and Are

> *Like a roasting*
> *Easter lamb,*
> *salted and seasoned,*
> *Christ fills our spirits*
> *with the aroma of hope.*

Telling the Story

"Mom, what are we going to do for Easter this year?" Maura's question pleased me deep inside of my soul. So often in our faith lives, our families only ask what we are going to do for Lent or some other penitential time. Maura's question felt like a gentle spring breeze, and I let it drift across my spirit for a moment before answering. Maura has a lot of the artist in her, and I wanted to know what, in her imagination, might be behind the question.

"What do you think, Maura? Do you have a picture of something you think would help all of us?"

"I do," she said. "You know how we usually place lilies around the house?"

"Yes" I replied.

"Well, this year, I would also like to have fresh herbs in every room, even in all of our bedrooms. I love their smell, and maybe we can even use some of them to flavor our food."

"That sounds wonderful, Maura, but why herbs at Easter?"

"Because I think Easter ought to flavor everything we are and do as Christians."

Her answer made me want to weep.

- ■ Can you think of a time when you wanted to weep in gratitude?

- ■ What is your dream for celebrating Easter at home?

Discovering the Meaning

I have spent hundreds of hours, both alone and with my family, trying to create an environment in our home that would help all of us penetrate the mystery of faith through ordinary things, such as flowers, rocks, wood, and water. When my children were small, we would work together decorating our home for each different season, as well as for the great feasts of the liturgical year. We hung colorful banners on our walls at the change of seasons, put a cactus and a few stones in the middle of the dining room table for Lent, yule wheels for Advent and Christmas, and a big bowl of water for Easter, just to name a few. We processed around our home to remember the journeys of the Magi, and formed huge circles of prayer with friends and family at picnics to mark the beginning and end of summer. Maura's suggestion for Easter was a small confirmation that authentic religion and faith are caught, not taught.

- How can you help family and friends catch faith?
- Take a moment, can you remember some special home ritual that really worked?

Acting

Think about what other people see when they enter your home. The decor doesn't have to be overflowing with religious symbols, but it does have to be inviting. How we welcome friends and family, especially children, is the ground upon which we build healthy faith relationships. Here are just a few questions we may ask ourselves in an effort to help create an environment where faith can prosper:

- Are there places for guests to sit down, relax, and feel comfortable?
- Do you have a room that is free of televisions, radios, telephones, and computers where everyone can talk without shouting, and listen without straining?

- Does the level of light invite everyone to be relaxed and enjoy one another's presence?

Faith, we must remember, does not happen all at once. Simply because we create a peaceful, inviting environment does not mean that people will automatically have a succession of serious conversations about faith or anything else. What it does mean is that everyone, even children, will know that the space we create for them is a place where important conversations, difficult questions, and joyful announcements can be made, freely and spontaneously. Creating an environment where everyone can peacefully gather and share faith stories is like turning over the ground in the strawberry patch (or any garden) and pulling up the weeds. Only then can we hope to plant flowers, plants, and herbs that will grow and bear fruit: things that will flavor our world!

In the early Church, Christians often gathered to pray and wait together in an all-night vigil for Easter morning. As they lit the candles, they told stories of the past, dreamed about the future, and focused on how they were experiencing God in the present. Reading about these gatherings, one wonders where and how they gathered and what these places looked like? What kind of environment did they create to offer a place of welcome, safety, and peace? What objects did they choose to create an atmosphere for prayer and storytelling?

In our home, we have a *Talking Shawl* which we pass from person to person at Easter. Like the *Talking Feather* of the Native peoples of the north where the person who holds the feather tells a story while the group listens, our shawl offers protection and warmth, inviting family members to tell their personal, family, and scriptural stories of hope with honesty and openness.

We also bake a special Easter bread using Maura's herbs. The bread's aroma permeates the entire house, creating a wonderful atmosphere for storytelling.

After everyone has had a chance to tell a story, we repeat a custom that comes to us from the Middle Ages, placing a candle in the middle of the bread. As each person holds the bread with the candle in the middle, everyone says a prayer of gratitude. Then, the bread is passed around, and each person breaks off a piece and eats it. Finally, the youngest children ring small bells as the *He Is Risen* story is told. In this way, Easter continues to flavor everything we do and are as Christians.

Remembering

Saint Paul says that our faith would be in vain if Jesus had not been raised from the dead. In the comic strip *Hip Shot*, Rick O'Shay says it this way: "Two big days for churchgoers, Christmas and Easter. But I think the second is the most important. Christmas is the promise, but Easter is the proof." Matthew's Gospel tells the story this way:

> After the sabbath, as the first day of the week was dawning, Mary Magdalene and the other Mary went to see the tomb. (…) But the angel said to the women, "Do not be afraid; I know that you are looking for Jesus who was crucified. He is not here; for he has been raised, as he said. Come, see the place where he lay." (…) So they left the tomb quickly with fear and great joy, and ran to tell his disciples. Suddenly Jesus met them and said, "Greetings!" And they came to him, took hold of his feet, and worshiped him. Then Jesus said to them, "Do not be afraid; go and tell my brothers to go to Galilee; there they will see me" (Mt 28:1, 5–6, 8–10).

Easter is a time to celebrate that Jesus has been raised from the dead, but like the two Marys, despite hearing Jesus tell us not to be afraid, we are, nonetheless, "half overjoyed, half fearful." The simple fact of the Resurrection takes time to fully enter our lives. The disciples, like the two Marys at the tomb of Jesus, were, at first, so stunned by the death of Jesus that they did not understand what was happening. Only with time did they realize that Jesus' promise to go before them to prepare a place did not mean preceding them to the earthly city of Jerusalem, but to the eternal Jerusalem. There would be no more death, no more dying, only waiting for the fullness of

Easter joy to fill every crevice of their lives. Like Maura said, Easter ought to flavor everything we do, but like fresh herbs, the flavor is subtle. Only gradually do their aroma and taste change where we live and what we eat. At the same time, the manner in which we let that flavor of Easter seep into everything we are is an indication of the authenticity of our faith. From our perspective, creating an inviting environment of peace in our homes is the best way to prepare for, and celebrate, our call to be an Easter people.

- How can we let the Easter event flavor everything we do and are?
- How can we bring the power of Easter into our daily lives?

Praying

God of All Flavors,
Create among, with, and in us, Easter God, safe environments, strawberry patches, atmospheres of peace, places of hope, and spaces of welcome where we gather and share faith stories, your story in us. Wrap a prayer shawl of protection and warmth around our shoulders as we enter into storytelling.

Turn over the ground of our life, pull up the weeds, plant and water us so that we become your herbs, flavoring everything we do and say with your life, Flavorful God. Let the aroma of herbs in the baking bread permeate our inner and outer home. We walk, talk, and have our being in the aroma of your love. We are your Easter people. Amen.

Suggested Ritual

Pass a container of blended fresh herbs for each person to smell and enjoy. People are invited to wear the talking shawl as they tell their story.

Down Time

Watching the puppies play
I yearned for freedom
And ached that my life
Seemed so full of emptiness.

Telling the Story

Brian, a third-grader, burst into my office.

Breathless, he asked: "Mrs. Cronin, I don't think I should stay for religious education this week. What do you think?"

"Why is that Brian?" I asked.

"I'm just too busy," he blurted, not able to look at me.

"What do you mean by 'too busy,' Brian?" I continued.

"Well, I have to leave class in a half hour. My mother is picking me up early so that we can get my grandmother, who is going to be staying with us while Mom and Dad go on a business trip. After we get Grandma, we need to pick up my sister, Amy, from soccer, go home, have a quick supper, and then drop me off for Little League tryouts. And I haven't even done my homework yet!"

By the time Brian finished his litany, I was breathless. Unfortunately, almost everyone who is involved with children can say the same thing. Children have no down time: no time to lie down under a tree, munch on an apple, and watch the clouds go by. Almost all of the children we know are involved in a multitude of extra activities that keep them so busy that they often seem anxious and distracted.

Because they are so afraid that their children will not measure up to other children, and they will be unfavorably compared to other parents, we suspect that parents permit, and even encourage, this "busyness" for their children. Accomplishment and success seem to have overtaken common sense.

- Are our children so busy that they think sitting quietly and playing is "boring"?
- If my child had to draw me, depicting my everyday life, what would she or he draw?

Discovering the Meaning

Like the cartoon character, the Road Runner, too many of us are constantly on the run, keyed up, checking lists, doing three things at once, almost running (beep, beep) to keep away from ourselves! At other times, like Alice in Wonderland, we run furiously, just to stay in place. Hurrying to the next event makes us ignore the violence that our rushing around does to our inner selves, the world around us, and the people we meet. The more we run, the more we lose touch with ourselves, and give in to the fear that our children will only value us if we do more and more for them, as well as everyone else.

In the south, we call dragonflies "mosquito hawks." I used to watch them sitting still on the wooden clothespins that held our wash on the line. Sometimes, I just sat and watched. Not only did I not want to disturb these fascinating multicolored insects, I was also afraid one of them might land on me. Watching dragonflies taught me an important lesson: if you sit still, your mind stops "hopping" from one thing to another, and your restless body learns to stay in the present moment. Watching dragonflies was a "downtime" for me. Children yearn for this in-between time when they don't have to make life happen, but can just sit back and let it happen.

- How can we assure our children have some "downtime" every day?
- What do we need to change, or let go of, in order to provide our children with time to sit still and just do nothing?

Acting

I remember a time years ago when my grandmother and I were walking to the store. Eager as I was to buy the food and get back home, I suddenly noticed that we were not taking our regular route. Even though I protested that this was the long way around, Grandma assured me that we would get to the store soon enough. Soon enough became a long time (according to my personal clock). Suddenly, we came upon the woods. Grandma and I stopped and sat on a rock, listening. The sound of the newly returned katydids filled the air. I was spellbound. Grandma smiled!

The long way around sometimes gifts us with an occasion for downtime. Downtime breaks the ground for contemplation, wonder, and play. It also allows us to recognize the poet within. Thomas Merton speaks of the need for our imagination to have "time to browse around." That's downtime.

Parents can model healthy behavior for children even as soon as they wake up in the morning. Taking a few moments to breathe deeply, greet the day, say a quiet prayer, and then begin breakfast preparations can be a wonderful invitation to children to enter days, classes, sports, and after-school activities more gently.

And when children return from school, we can help them have their own downtime. Ask your children to "image" a calm place—a field, a pond, or woods—and mentally go there to rest. With a little practice, they will even look forward to their downtime.

Simple exercises like puttering around, strolling, gardening, drawing, moving toy cars through villages under backyard trees, fishing without bait on the hook, watching the clouds, and even taking a nap all foster downtime which can lead a person to reflection, livelier conversations, and even prayer. Though it takes practice, downtime is a skill we all need to learn. Someone once wrote the following:

> *Most of the time, it*
> *is fun to play with*
> *other children or to*
> *be with grownups,*
> *but sometimes you just*
> *want everyone*
> *to leave you alone.*
> *Then it is a good thing*
> *to have a little house*
> *of your own—*
> *a secret house,*
> *under a dining room*
> *table can be a*
> *secret house*
> *or behind a chair in a corner.*
> *And there's one thing*
> *to remember. If you*
> *should be walking*
> *near somebody's*
> *little house, walk*
> *softly, walk gently.*

Remembering

In a world so full of "doing," we wonder whether children will ever be able to hear Jesus say: "Come to me all you who are heavy burdened and I will refresh you." Jesus' willingness to welcome us as we are, even in our "busyness," is a foundational gospel value. We need to take time to hear him when he reminds us:

> "Therefore I tell you, do not worry about your life, what you will eat or what you will drink, or about your body, what you will wear. Is not life more than food, and the body more than clothing? Look at the birds of the air; they neither sow nor reap nor gather into barns, and yet your heavenly Father feeds them. Are you not of more value than they? And can

any of you by worrying add a single hour to your span of life? (...) Therefore do not worry, saying, 'What will we eat?'or 'What will we drink?' or 'What will we wear?' (...) So do not worry about tomorrow, for tomorrow will bring worries of its own. Today's trouble is enough for today" (Mt 6:25–27, 31, 34).

The Jews of Jesus' era were like a "second world" people. Although their nation had a name, it had no real independence because the Romans conquered, taxed, and still governed them. Not surprisingly, they often worried about whether they would have enough on which to live. But the Lord assured them that their identity and value were not rooted in how much land they owned, nor how many children they had, but in the simple fact that God calls them his beloved people, and he would always accompany them on all their journeys. And today, God assures us that this is still true.

- Is our trust in God strong enough to sustain us in times of trial?
- What can we do, today, on a daily basis, to strengthen our faith?

Praying

God of Dragonflies, Katydids, and Birds of the Air,
Calm our hopping feet and minds. Like the cartoon character the Road Runner, we rush through life, either running away from or towards something. We are always on the move. Our restless spirits have left no room for your Presence, so filled are we with getting more and more and even more. There is a violence to our rushing. Guide us to a resting-in-you place: a field, a pond, a woods, a secret house under a table or behind a chair, a calm place to rest. Give us, Creator God, some downtime, an in-between time, so we can browse around slowly together. Amen.

Suggested Ritual

Take a few quiet moments. Hear God speak this breath prayer over and over again in you:

Breathe in and hear: Be still.
Breathe out and hear: I am with you.

The Habit of Gratitude

Do we,
Like earth, sky, wind and ocean,
Sing and dance everyday
In gratitude
For who we are?

Telling the Story

Sarah's face was aglow. No longer the frenetic little three-year-old who tore the wrappings off her birthday presents, she was now five, and took her time with each gift. I was amazed just watching her. After examining each gift for a long time, she went to the person who had given it, looked directly into their eyes and thanked them with a big hug. I kept expecting her to grow tired, but was pleasantly surprised by her patience and care. She never rushed, but took the time to treasure each gift, and seemed genuinely touched by the attention shown her.

Though Sarah was not able to maintain her "contemplative presence" throughout her entire party, she had already learned so much about how to live gently on the earth. When children are taught to express gratitude regularly, they grow socially and spiritually as well. Sarah, the oldest of my grandchildren, has been a caring mentor to her younger siblings and cousins. Her teachers also notice her kind spirit, and tell her parents how grateful they are for Sarah's goodness. Sarah's gratitude, they say, is contagious and changes the environment in their classrooms.

- Do you take time each day to be grateful for life's simple gifts?
- When you do take time for gratitude, how does it change you?

Discovering the Meaning

Gratitude enlarges the heart and unlocks the fullness of life. The power of gratitude catches us by surprise. It awakens and transforms us. By treasuring simple, everyday gifts, we are nourished and made full. We taste and see the goodness of the Lord, even in difficult times. Sarah has taught me this and so has my six-year-old niece.

When Kett's three years of chemotherapy finally ended, we rejoiced. My sister made a special cake, served it with ice cream, and gave her daughter two balloons. Kett held onto those balloons all week, protecting and caring for them. On Friday, she asked her mother if they could visit Grandpa. As soon as Kett saw her grandfather, she handed him one of her precious balloons, kissed him, and said: "We were good, Grandpa. Everything will be fine now." That Friday had marked the last day of her grandfather's radiation treatments.

Gifts as simple as balloons remind us to focus, not on what we lack, but celebrate the abundance of what we have. Though lacking good health, Kett gave from her abundance. Like Kett, our children are naturally inclined to express their gratitude. By listening to their innate goodness, we can learn to do the same.

- Do we sometimes take the simple gift of life for granted?
- Do we regularly tell stories of gratitude to our children and other family members?

Acting

Parents can help their children develop an "attitude of gratitude" simply by companioning them. Rachel Carson, in *The Sense of Wonder*, reminds us: "If a child is to keep alive an inborn sense of wonder, s/he needs the companionship of at least one adult who can share it, rediscovering with him (or her) the joy, excitement, and mystery of the world in which we live."

As adults, we have the privilege of walking with our children, teaching them, by example, not to take life and its treasures for granted. When children see their parents honoring creation, each other, and them through the quality of their caring behaviors, they become grounded in gratitude. Taking a leisurely walk with children and grandchildren through a park, a zoo, or even in your own neighborhood can be a wonderful lesson in gratitude. Stopping to appreciate flowers, insects, the sky, and letting ourselves feel the wind in our faces can help children see our reverence for creation and all God's gifts. By focusing on abundance and appreciating what we have, we weave gratitude into the fabric of our daily lives.

Julian of Norwich teaches a similar lesson: "God is all that is good and the goodness that everything has, is God." In the play about her life, Julian utters these words: "Listen. Birds sing. The sun shines. There is freshness in the air. And look the river winds in the distance. Sparrows, pigeons, dogs and cats, people, all gifts of our loving maker." We really are rich beyond belief! We have adequate food, clean water, schools, medical care, and the freedom to pursue our goals. When we take these gifts for granted, we cheat our children of the great grace of exuberance. Children are often bursting to say: "Thank you, God. You are wonderful!" Helping our children create simple rituals of gratefulness reminds everyone to remember how great God is, and how fortunate we are.

With practice, gratitude can become a habit. Families might keep a record of the blessings they receive. Writing them down or drawing in a "gratitude book" each day helps us remember how good God is. These seemingly insignificant blessings could be whatever helped family members feel good about themselves each day. That is what gifts do! We might write or draw about

- a smile in the school hallway
- the smell of wet mud after a morning rain shower
- our first cup of morning coffee
- wildflowers in a calico vase
- Grandpa telling a story about me
- jelly beans in a jar
- a child noticing and smelling a newly opened rose
- being trusted

- mint cookies
- a nap

Gratitude that is deeply planted in our hearts changes how we see the world and one another. Helping children practice gratitude early in life helps them grow in self-respect and in a spirit of service. There are few virtues more important than gratitude.

Remembering

Life itself, especially in the face of life-threatening illness, is a great gift. Jesus says it this way: "I came that they may have life, and have it abundantly" (Jn 10:10). And Saint Paul, in his letter to the Colossians, reminds us:

> And let the peace of Christ rule in your hearts, to which indeed you were called in the one body. And be thankful. Let the word of Christ dwell in you richly; teach and admonish one another in all wisdom; and with gratitude in your hearts sing psalms, hymns, and spiritual songs to God. And whatever you do, in word or deed, do everything in the name of the Lord Jesus, giving thanks to God the Father through him (Col 3:15–17).

Even though Paul challenges the church in Colossae to be full of gratitude, despite the struggles of proclaiming the Gospel amidst the difficulties of daily life, we often take that gift of life for granted, and forget to learn the lessons that both Sarah and Kett teach us. Life is an incalculable gift to be treasured every day. Gratitude for life should be given away as freely as the gift itself has been give to us.

- How can we maintain inner peace in our lives?
- How can we remain grateful when we are faced with difficulties?

Praying

God of All Goodness,
   We gasp, surprised by the everyday gifts of cake, ice cream, and balloons, which celebrate the abundance of who we are, and what we have. Like the child, Kett, release us, Gift Giving God, to give from our abundance; to treasure each gift we receive with the patience and care of the six-year-old Sarah; and to proclaim with the mystic, Julian, "God is all that is good and the goodness that everything has is God." Wonder-full God, companion us into your delight and mystery. Weave gratitude into the ordinary fabric of our lives and days. Let us, "like earth, sky, wind, and ocean—sing and dance every day in gratitude." Amen.

Suggested Ritual

You may want to gather with your family to speak a blessing prayer of gratitude. Take a few moments to recall the treasures of what you saw, heard, and received today. Together as one people (God's people), take turns naming a gift out loud, the group responds: *yes, yes, yes!* When everyone has had an opportunity to share, invite them to stand up and bow in reverence to the totality of all life.

III

Watering the Garden
■ ■ ■

"For I will pour water on the thirsty land, and streams on the dry ground...."
                                                                                    ISAIAH 44:3

Focus

When someone takes notice that we are thirsty or lonely, it eases our pain. At the same time, we cannot allow ourselves to forget that if we cannot find, get, or give the water of compassion to others, we will all die. Some will die from thirst, others will die from drowning, still others will die when they realize they have no one with whom to share their strawberries.

Nothing can live without water. Nothing: no plants, animals, insects, nor humans. Nevertheless, most of the world continues to suffer without clean water. This simple tragedy, apparent to anyone who has ever had to travel through or live in the Third World, ought to make us pause to reflect for a moment. While we should always glory in the beauty of cascading water falls and tumbling oceans, and because it is our nature to be just and compassionate, we also want to bring clean water to all God's creatures. With Jeremiah, we can say: "...I will let them walk by brooks of water, / in a straight path in which they shall not stumble..." (Jer 31:9).

How shall we water the garden of faith? How can we pass on the great truths of our religious tradition? Let us pray while we read the following four essays for the strength to grieve our losses and to be able to accompany others during their own. In a world that is sometimes swallowed by greed, let us act with conviction and determination to live the symbols of our baptism in our daily lives. Touch, stroke, clothe, and water those who have nothing. There is no more powerful way to make our faith come alive.

Reflections

In watering the garden of faith:

- ■ How do we listen to what our family tells us of their times of sadness and joy?
- ■ Who listens to us with compassion when we are fearful of loss, failure, or death?
- ■ Where do you go for healing?
- ■ How does Jesus weep with us when we grieve?

Dealing With Fear

Exhausted eyes
stare at us
from every hungry child
challenging us
to change.

Telling the Story

Fear can paralyze us. A few weeks ago, my daughter Claire called and was very upset. Sarah, her then three-year-old, was on the verge of dehydration due to illness. If Sarah could not drink one quart of liquid within the next hour, she would be placed in the hospital. As soon as I arrived at their home, Claire left to bring her three-week-old infant Maggie, who was also ill, to the doctor.

As I looked at Sarah, my first grandchild, my heart ached. I sat down beside her. We talked:

"Could you try to drink some of this red juice?"

"No, Grandma, I'm afraid. It hurts my tummy too much and I'll throw up."

I held her in my arms. "Sarah, sometimes we have to do things that hurt, but are good for us. This takes a lot of courage."

"Where do you get courage, Grandma?" Sarah asked.

"It's inside you already," I said, "but sometimes it is hard to find."

A few moments later, I suggested we sing. Holding and rocking Sarah, I whispered a song. When I finished, I held up the juice and she took a few sips. No words were spoken. During the next hour, her courage awakened and she finished the quart of liquid.

Three months later, Sarah came to me and said she had given her "binkie" to the fairy. But she was sad and afraid to sleep at night without it. She wanted her binkie back. I reminded her about the hard things in life and our talk about courage.

"I remember, Grandma, when I had courage and drank that red juice."

I said, "Tonight, you will find courage inside again. Remember how God helped you."

She turned to me and smiled. "That's true, Grandma, but you helped me too, because you were there."

In the midst of my own fears and darkness, this little child reminded me that we need not be alone in our fears. If we speak of our fears, and let someone be with us, our fears almost always diminish.

■ How often do we take a moment to be grateful for those times when fear did not overwhelm us, and faith sustained us?

Discovering the Meaning

When Jack's mother died, he spoke of the haunting reservoir of emptiness he felt. In trying to attend to and sit with his loss, he discovered something else. Even though he had been a priest for more than twenty-five years and had prayed with countless dying people, he was still profoundly afraid of death. Though he was embarrassed, identifying and giving a name to his fear helped him grow in compassion, especially for the children he knows and teaches. This kind of empathy is exactly what children (or adults, for that matter) really need when they are afraid.

While it is tempting to instruct children about a God who frees us from fear, that is not what they really require. Children need compassionate adult friends and companions, not more instruction about the mystery of loss and death. They need people who will walk with them, and hold them when they need that assurance. They do not need people who are trying to convince them that death is nothing to fear because the Lord has gone before us to prepare a place. When we allow ourselves to feel the fear that swims around in all of us, especially during periods of transition and acute loss, we assure friends, family, and children that we are in need of more than an intellectual conviction about the gift of eternal life. We are sending them an invitation to walk with and hold us when nothing makes sense, except their faith-filled touch. More important, for them, we become a gift of honesty, integrity, and hope.

Moreover, since we know that fear prevents mature responsible action, part of the process of growing up is learning to identify the different kinds of fear we feel, and distinguish among them. Additionally, when children discover that some fears can be outgrown, they begin to separate the real fears from the imaginary ones.

Psychologists speak about two kinds of fear. The first is a *fear of consequences*: the fear of what it will cost us by way of involvement and risk, and of what others will say or do in response to something we have done. The second is the *fear of failure*: afraid to make a mistake, we wonder why we are not "good enough" for a particular school or group, and the feeling that we don't measure up to our own, or other peoples', expectations. When young people become discouraged, failure can seem greater to them than it really is. Like us adults, they sometimes tend to run from a threatening situation, not confronting or dealing with it directly. In either case, fear is a defensive reaction which causes us to close ourselves to others, to the real community. If we are too afraid that others will hurt us, we can never be free enough to really care for them.

The strawberry patch teaches us the same lesson. When we are tempted by fear, anxiety, or confusion and want to cut ourselves off from everyone else to survive, we must stay connected. Don't give in to the fear. Though we may go underground for a while, as long as we remain connected to one another in faith God will be our guide and strength.

- ■ How can we help our children face and name their fears?
- ■ How can faith help us do this?

Acting

Sometimes, people are embarrassed about being afraid and pretend that they aren't. In the story, *The King and I*, Anna reminds her son that whenever he feels afraid, he should "hold his head up high and whistle a happy tune." You can convince yourself that you are not afraid, she insists, so that "when you fool the people you fool, you fool yourself instead." While this might work sometimes, our children need to know that it is OK to be afraid of things they don't understand, unknown places, and things that might hurt them. It's OK to want to get away from things that scare them. And when they are afraid, they shouldn't pretend they are not.

Fear can be a warning that we are in danger and need to be careful. It is good to tell someone else about what scares us, and find out about the things we fear by asking questions. We might even find out that we don't need to be afraid, or that fear is the proper response. Fear is with us in so many ways that, unless we find ways to attend to it, make friends with it, and move through it together with our children, we can never be free. How, then, do we begin to handle our fears? In our home, we strive to do several of the following things:

- *Be aware* of the fear—Recognize that fear is present and pay attention to it.
- *Admit* to feeling fear—Try to name it, and tell someone about it.
- *Reflect*—Try to understand why we are afraid, and ask questions to find out about the things that frighten us.
- *Decide*—Take into account the danger which is making us afraid.
- *Pray*—Sometimes, we have to make friends with our fears, even picturing ourselves holding a particular fear in our hand, and asking it to tell us its story. Pray that God will help us release our inner courage to deal with it.

It can also be helpful for us to draw a picture of what frightened us when we were younger, or what frightens us now. This can be a springboard to discussion among all family members. The invitation to tell a story, or share an experience that frightened us, welcomes each person to see how fear is a part of everyone's lives.

Remembering

The Scriptures speak about two kinds of fear. The first, a fear of God, is holy, filling us with awe and wonder at God's greatness and love, despite our failings. But the gospel reminds us that Jesus wants to free us from the second kind of fear, the one that paralyzes us with doubt and anxiety. In Luke's Gospel, we read:

> "I tell you, my friends, do not fear those who kill the body, and after that can do nothing more. (...) Are not five sparrows sold for two pennies? Yet not one of them is forgotten in God's sight. (...) Do not be afraid; you are of more value than many sparrows" (Lk 12:4, 6–7).

What a great and generous God we have! While God promises us that fear will not last forever, we also read that Jesus himself was full of great fear as he approached his passion and death:

> Then Jesus went with them to a place called Gethsemane; and he said to his disciples, "Sit here while I go over there and pray." (...) Then he said to them, "I am deeply grieved, even to death; remain here, and stay awake with me." And going a little farther, he threw himself on the ground and prayed, "My Father, if it is possible, let this cup pass from me; yet not what I want but what you want" (Mt 26:36, 38–39).

The Gospel assures us that Jesus accompanies us fully in our humanity, feeling fear, sorrow, and loss. In this way, Jesus promises us, despite our everyday fears, he will always be with us.

The phrase "Do not be afraid" occurs more than 365 times in the Bible. That not only tells us that there is much fear in our world, but also that God is on a mission to help us to be free. When the angels speak to Mary, Joseph, the shepherds, and to the women at the tomb, they say: "Be not afraid." Even before asking what they want, Jesus says to the blind man, the lame, the daughters of Sion:

"Do not be afraid." And, on Pentecost, we again hear these words spoken to the men and women who are huddled behind locked doors, afraid for their lives: "Be not afraid, I am with you." Helping our children handle their fears is a way we pass our faith on to them.

- Do we honestly believe that Jesus felt fear just like we do?
- Are we able to pray in the midst of fear? Or can we simply offer our fear as a prayer to God?

Praying

God of Fearlessness,

Hold me. Rock me in your arms, Gentle One. Let me hear your whispering song: "You are not alone. I am here." Awaken my courage. I feel like I am swimming in all-encompassing feelings that overwhelm me.

Fear sometimes paralyzes me. Nothing seems to make any sense. Help me face and name my fear. Let me know that it's OK to be afraid.

Surround me with companions who will be with me as I try gently to hold my fear in my hands and ask it to tell me its story. Through and in my darkness, help me grow in compassion and empathy for others who are entangled in a net of fear. May all of your creation hear your gentle voice: "Be not afraid. I am with you." Amen.

Suggested Ritual

Imagine your loved ones surrounding you. Sit quietly. Acknowledge your fear and gently hold it in your hands, asking and waiting for it to tell you its story. Allow some time for this movement. Then invite the other people present to offer a hug and whisper: *I will be your companion. You are not alone. God walks with us.*

Divorce: Offering Healing When Everything Hurts

*Christmas isn't about gifts
Unless you don't have any to give
or get.*

Telling the Story

"Only fifteen shopping days left 'til Christmas, Mom. Hope you have everything on my list!" Beth blanched when she heard her oldest daughter say this phrase. She had managed to scrape together enough money to get all the gifts her children requested that first Christmas after Tom left. But now another Christmas was almost here again, and she could not possibly satisfy all their "needs."

Some days, she felt overwhelmed. Although her parents and siblings had been very supportive, and she had joined Parents Without Partners, she had less money, fewer friends, and much less self-confidence. Even if she could buy her children everything they wanted, she was not sure she could ever offer them the strength and faith they really needed. In fact, she wasn't sure she possessed them herself!

Beth had anticipated everything but this. Faith had always been the ground upon which she built her life. Even when she wasn't feeling well, she could turn to prayer and discover God's peace. Now, even this consolation was beginning to fail her! Not only was she worried, she was feeling a kind of darkness she had never known. Never one to seek counsel, she knew she needed to speak with someone, but wasn't sure where or to whom she might turn. Her confusion was turning into panic. Where could she go? To whom might she speak?

- How does Beth's story affect you?

- What would you say to her if she were here with you right now?

Discovering the Meaning

Christmas, from a faith perspective, is one of the most beautiful times of the liturgical year. We light candles, sing delightful songs, and work at paying more attention to others than ourselves. Nevertheless, there are times in our lives when we feel so battered that it is difficult not to become self-absorbed. Separation and divorce are just two of the life-altering events that leave both adults and children feeling empty, lost, and confused. Beth knew all of these feelings and was struggling to find a path out of her darkness. She, her children, and her estranged husband are just a few of the people to whom we are called in a special way at Christmas. Jesus says it plainly: "No one after lighting a lamp puts it under the bushel basket, but on the lampstand, and it gives light to all in the house" (Mt 5:15).

Christmas is about sharing the light of faith with all people, especially the children of divorce who feel lost and abandoned because of it. Beth and her family invite us to break out of our comfortable world to recognize, respond, and care for those most in need. Especially when we are feeling very blessed, we have an opportunity to stand with those who ask nothing more than for us to become a wall against which they can lean for a while to catch their spirit's breath.

Several years ago, a group of teenage girls on a camping trip taught me this very same lesson. Huddling together in a lean-to late one evening, the sounds of the night had disturbed their sleep. In the darkness, they found their way to my lean-to, where the remaining embers of a campfire still burned. Frightened, the girls had come to my makeshift dwelling for protection and refuge. Feeling like strangers in a strange land, it was as if they almost shouted: "We don't fit here. We don't know what to do. Take us home." We can almost hear Beth and her children saying the same thing. They need us to be a lean-to for them as they walk in darkness. The following prayer of a young child might help them all:

Some days, friend Jesus,
I just don't fit.
Other kids tease me.
They make fun of my weight.
They ignore me. They laugh at me.
I just don't fit.
They whisper behind my back.
They won't let me into their group.
I just don't fit.

Some kids are smart
   and others make jokes about them.
Some kids have trouble in school
   and others make fun of them.
I just don't fit.
My favorite pants don't fit anymore.
I've grown and shoes don't fit.

Help me to remember that
   in your love, Jesus,
I fit.

I always have and I always will.
(*Friend Jesus*, Saint Anthony, 2000)

- How and when are we a wall, or a lean-to, for our children?
- How can we respond to our children when they feel that they "just don't fit"?

Acting

One of the most difficult moments for suffering people, especially children, emerges when they wonder what others think of them. Guilt and shame often mark their grief. Beth and her children were very concerned about whether they would be accepted by others at school, in their neighborhood, and at church. And Beth wasn't sure whether she would be invited to teach religious education again. More important, Beth and her children questioned what it meant to be family. Every time they gathered together for a meal, they stared at the empty chair. Haunted by their pain, they wanted to be the same as everyone else, but felt very different. Their grief and loss were deeply seeded. Like the whiteouts that winter storms sometimes bring, they were unable to discern the various shapes of God on the horizon. It was dark and frightening being "strangers in a strange land," where nothing fits any longer.

We can help Beth, her family, and others like her simply by standing with them without judgment. What a wonderful sign of holy affection we can offer the divorced, and their children, when we encourage our children and grandchildren to play together with them. It is also important to include the children of the divorced in special Christmas celebrations and pageants, and offer them a community with whom to share Christmas. Of course, this needs to be done with special care, but the delicacy of the matter should not deter us from taking action. Children need to feel that they are not the cause of their parents' difficulties. By making sure to include them in Christmas celebrations, we assure them of our love in the midst of the pain they feel.

Remembering

Don't we all need the Church to be like a burning ember: "…a lamp shining in a dark place, until the day dawns and the morning star rises in your hearts" (2 Pet 1:19)? When Peter was writing his letter, he knew that the Church was experiencing a terrible weakness of faith. Confused by the internal bickering about how to live the gospel in a non-Jewish world, and overwhelmed by philosophical questions from the Gentile world, they wondered about their own role. To be "a lamp shining in a dark place" is Peter's only request. Lamps help others see. They are not invasive, and they don't tell us what to see, or how to see it. Only God can do that. Today, be a light for others. Surely, that will be enough.

- ■ How can we be lights for our children in a very confusing world?

- Take a gratitude moment to remember someone who was a light for you as a child. Have you thanked them recently? Or even told them how important they were to you and your family?

Praying

Lean-to God,

The night sounds have disturbed our sleep. Darkness surrounds us. Feelings of loss, grief, and abandonment fill this night space. We hear the aching voices of friends who are going through separation and divorce, crying out for your gifts of strength and faith. They feel like strangers in a strange land. Nothing fits, they tell us. They yearn for home again.

Make us become a lean-to for others as they walk in darkness and try to catch their spirit's breath. Like teenage girls on a camping trip make us into your make-shift dwellings of protection and refuge for others. Let us stand with them without judgment, and be your sign of holy affection. Like the remaining burning ember of a campfire, help us offer light and warmth. Our eyes are on you, God, until the first streaks of dawn appear and you, the Morning Star, rise in our hearts. Huddle with us, Gracious One, in every lean-to of our life. Amen.

Suggested Ritual

You may want to place an empty chair at the table. In silence, name and unite yourself with people who are struggling with a void in their lives. In prayer, imagine them sitting at the table. Become a lean-to for another person in need.

Death: Saying Good-Bye

Anger,
like a searing blast of summer heat,
almost knocks me over
with sadness.

Telling the Story

Tara was fourteen when her grandfather died. With some embarrassment, even guilt, she realized that her first reaction to her grandfather's death was relief. Tara's granddad had been suffering from a violent form of cancer, one that stole pounds from his already thin body, and caused him great pain. Her relief, she realized, meant that he no longer had to suffer, and she was happy for him.

Only afterward did Tara begin to feel angry. At times, she was angry at her mother. At other times, she wanted to scream at her younger brother. She felt terribly lonely and confused. Unfortunately, her anger only made her feel even more guilty. She knew she wasn't really mad at her mother or brother, but not knowing how to express her grief, she misdirected it for a while. Finally, several weeks after her grandfather's burial, realizing she would never see him again, she begin to cry and release the pain and loss she felt.

Several months later, Tara visited her grandmother. Even though the pain she experienced was still raw, she felt more in control. Sitting with her grandmother, she noticed one of her grandfather's favorite old sweaters and asked if she could have it. Handing Tara the sweater, her grandmother suggested it might be God's way of helping her believe that her grandfather would always have his arms around her. Tara knew she would wear that sweater often.

- Has someone close to you died?
- Did you feel anger?
- How did you grieve?

- If they had been ill, did you experience the confusion of feeling grief when they died? How did you handle that emotion?

Discovering the Meaning

Even though our society has a tendency to dress death up to make it look like sleep, children often feel its sting very deeply. They need a safe place where they can feel free to express their grief. Having sensitive grandmothers like Tara's can help, but children also need to be hugged often during their time of grieving. Words are not sufficient when their belief that the world is a safe place is threatened by death.

Our own grief can also get in the way of being present to our own children and grandchildren. Recently, while praying with a family whose eldest son and brother had died tragically, I became acutely aware of the confusion my friend's grandchildren were feeling. While their aunts and uncles cried, and tried to put words around their grief, I noticed the children's eyes darting from adult to adult. Instinctively responding to their fear, all the adults joined hands and reached out to them. Then, their grandmother, smiling gently, spoke very softly: "We are very sad today. Losing Uncle Michael hurts all of us. Even though we know he is with God, we are afraid and sad. Crying at times like this is very natural, and it helps us. When we remember to support one another like this, we know we'll be OK." No one spoke for a while. Then, everyone hugged the children tightly.

- How can you show tenderness to children experiencing the death of a loved one?
- Is it possible to be more "real" about death with children?

Acting

In *Stray Birds,* the poet Tagore says, "Death belongs to life as birth does. The walk is in the raising of the foot as in the laying of it down." Recognizing this truth, there are some simple guidelines for being present to a grieving child:

1. We try to avoid phrases like grandpa has "passed on" or "gone to sleep." Not only do these euphemisms confuse children, they can make them afraid of falling asleep.
2. We try to tell our children that nothing they did caused the person to die.
3. We work with them to help find healthy ways to express their anger. If discipline is needed during this grieving time, we offer it with compassion and firmness. It doesn't help either party to ignore a child's behavior or relax all the rules.

Families would do well to mark anniversaries of deaths with simple rituals. Offering children opportunities for playing the game "I remember when..." and looking together at photographs of the person who died can be very helpful. Every year on my father's anniversary, I place his picture, with a candle burning in front of it, on the kitchen table. It's a photo of Dad standing in front of a "widgeon," an airplane he modified so that it could fly faster into the Gulf of Mexico on rescue missions during severe storms. The photo evokes a bushel of memories for me, some of them painful. It also invites family members to speak about "Grandpa," and what he meant to each person. This simple ritual not only reminds everyone that our ancestors really do live in our memories and good deeds, but it also helps us to let go of any lingering hurt, while still honoring that person and God.

Remembering

The eleventh chapter of John's Gospel tells us about Mary, the sister of Lazarus, who is both angry and hurt by the Lord when he fails to heal her sick brother:

> When Mary came where Jesus was and saw him, she knelt at his feet and said to him, "Lord, if you had been here, my brother would not have died." When Jesus saw her weeping, and the Jews who came with her also weeping, he was greatly

disturbed in spirit and deeply moved. He said, "Where have you laid him?" They said to him, "Lord, come and see." Jesus began to weep (Jn 11:32–35).

Death is not an easy event to handle at any time, even in the ancient world, where lower life expectancies forced people to face death on a much more regular basis than we do. While Mary's grief and anger seems to startle Jesus, his tears of compassion for her and her sister, Martha, assure them and us both that he understands. The humanity of Jesus is rarely portrayed more dramatically than in this story. It powerfully reminds us that grieving is both a natural and necessary part of life.

- How do we feel knowing that Jesus wept for his friend and his family?
- What does that tell you about Jesus for your own life?
- How does your family handle death?
- What can you do to help families face death with faith?

Praying

God of All Good-Byes,
There is an ache inside that seems to grow bigger and bigger, making breathing become difficult when it is time to say good-bye. Sadness fills every nook and cranny of my being. As you were with Mary and Martha, grieving over the death of their brother and your friend Lazarus, be startled by my tears and, in your compassion, weep with me over my own loss. Release the pain. I am so lonely and confused. Teach me to grieve and be present to others in their losses. Hug me in my confusion and loneliness. Like Tara wearing her grandfather's old sweater, reminding her of his presence, wrap me with the shawl of memory.

Tell me, Compassionate One, that the people I love who have died will always be a part of me. Their love and spirit will walk with me. I close my eyes and feel the connection, experiencing their guidance and help. Be my place of refuge, God, as I say good-bye and hello. Amen.

Suggested Ritual

Wrap yourself in a shawl. Light a candle. In the warmth of its flame, relate stories of your most recent good-bye to a person you love. Hold something that belonged to that person or have a photograph of the person before you.

Frozen Feelings

*As fearful as a young lion,
the divorced child
watches and waits,
wondering whether to pounce
or run.*

Telling the Story

Byron was almost seven when his grandmother brought him to our religious-education program to prepare for first Eucharist. Quiet, almost sullen, Byron was also mean. With adults, he was reasonably responsive, but with other children, he said very little, and rarely took part in class activities. The other children were afraid of him. Whenever his teacher was busy with another child, Byron would poke, tease, or threaten any child near him. Soon, he had his own way. The other children stayed far away from him, and a teacher's aide watched him constantly.

When I called Byron's grandmother to tell her about his behavior in class, she protested. Byron was a gentle child at home she insisted. He loved to watch television and would sit for hours with his grandfather watching sports. She couldn't understand his behavior in school. After a few minutes of conversation, Byron's grandmother wondered if his mother's two divorces, as well as his own separation from his siblings, might be the cause of his struggles. Byron, she told me, was the youngest child of her youngest daughter. When Byron was three, her daughter was hospitalized for nervous exhaustion. At that time, Byron and his three brothers lived with their grandmother for three months. When Byron's mother was released from the hospital, Byron's siblings returned home, but he stayed with his grandparents.

- What does violence do to your spirit?
- How do you respond?

- Do you really know the entirety of other people's stories?
- How do you manage feelings of abandonment in your own life?

Discovering the Meaning

People in "twelve step" spirituality-based groups, such as Al-Anon, speak of children like Byron having "frozen feelings." Because they have so often been locked into patterns of abandonment and shame, their feelings of gentleness, compassion, and openness "freeze." They become cold, distant, and impenetrable. While they may appear normal in tightly controlled situations, they often act out angrily when they are expected to risk new relationships. While children as fragile as Byron may be relatively few, every experienced religious educator has endured the pain of trying to accept and draw children like Byron out of themselves.

- Do you have frozen places within you?
- How can you "thaw" them?

Acting

Before parents and teachers can hope to respond to Byron and other children like him, we first need to face our own frozen feelings. Very few of us are without areas in our inner lives that do not need healing. If we were abused in any way as children, experienced the pain of a failed marriage, or watched a child slip into an addiction, we know what it means to become cold, distant, and angry. The hurt of losing the people upon whom we depend for nurturing and meaning can be overwhelming. When we identify and give a name to these feelings, accept them, and ask for the strength to move beyond them into healing, we are ready to live a life of compassion towards others, like Byron, who have no skills, and often no religious tradition to help them face the terror of abandonment and the loss of parents, friends, and mentors.

Recently, a young girl was sent to my office. The note she carried said "inappropriate behavior in class." She told me that she was bored. I paused. The word "bored" coming from my own children, grandchildren, and students sets off an alarm in me. Calmly, I asked her to spend a moment thinking about how being "bored" feels. She picked up a book from my desk and began to flip through it. I waited. Finally, when she let herself feel "bored," she realized how angry she was with her brother. Her feelings of being bored were a way to survive and cope with her real hurt feelings. If she showed her anger, she might have displeased her parents or given her brother a reason to hit her.

All behavior happens for a reason. We need to help our children recognize, name, and feel their feelings in order to get to the real story behind them. As a helping exercise, you can ask them to imagine holding their feelings gently in their hands. You might also ask how they need you to help care for their feelings until they are ready to speak about them. Getting to the story behind the feelings is the key to unlocking the warmth needed to thaw them.

When we recognize and accept one another's feelings in our homes, we provide an environment that fosters honesty in their expression. You might want to make "feeling cards," and place them, face down, on a table. Each person then draws a card that has a feeling word written on it. Then, each person speaks about a situation when they feel lonely, afraid, put down, angry, happy, or secure. Everyone else simply listens to the person speaking without passing judgment. By listening openly to one another, we help everyone accept their feelings, tell the stories behind them, and thaw the frozen ones.

Remembering

Our Scriptures are full of people like Byron. While there are many stories about people with troubled spirits who may have been afflicted with "frozen feelings," it is the story of Thomas that strikes us most powerfully as that of a person who was so hurt by the loss of Jesus that he stopped feeling:

But Thomas (who was called the Twin), one of the twelve, was not with them when Jesus came. So the other disciples told him, "We have seen the Lord." But he said to them, "Unless I see the mark of the nails in his hands, and put my finger in the mark of the nails and my hand in his side, I will not believe." A week later his disciples were again in the house, and Thomas was with them. Although the doors were shut, Jesus came and stood among them and said, "Peace be with you." Then he said to Thomas, "Put your finger here and see my hands. Reach out your hand and put it in my side. Do not doubt but believe." Thomas answered him, "My Lord and my God!" Jesus said to him, "Have you believed because you have seen me? Blessed are those who have not seen and yet have come to believe" (Jn 20:24–29).

Shame is a terrible feeling. One feels unworthy of any respect or love. The culture into which Jesus was born was a shame-based one. The young couple who had no wine for their wedding, and lepers who were unable to join their families, even on the biggest of feasts, were full of shame, and Jesus reaches out to them. He extends his hand to Thomas in the same way.

Because Thomas was not with the apostles when Jesus first appeared to them after the Resurrection, and perhaps because he was too hurt to even associate with his closest friends, he reacted angrily to the story of Jesus' Resurrection. "Unless I put my hand into his side and fingers into the nail marks in his hand, I will not believe." When Jesus appeared to his friends a second time, he invited Thomas to let go of his hurt and disillusionment, and become an exuberant believer again. Lifted out of his emptiness by the Lord's graciousness, Thomas is reminded: "You believed because you saw. Blessed are they who have not seen and yet believe." These last words of Jesus might be addressed to all of us as we try, with steady warmth, to reach out to the abandoned, destitute, and lonely people, like Byron, to help them believe again, and thaw their frozen feelings.

- Have you ever been so hurt that you wanted to pull away from everything you believed?
- How did you respond? Did faith help or hurt?
- Do you know people who are so hurt or shame-filled that they withdraw, even from their closest friends?
- How can you help them?

Praying

Gracious God,

Shelter us in the warmth of your love and thaw our frozen feelings. Lift us out of our emptiness. Make us unafraid to awaken our feelings by naming and simply being with them, both the pleasant and unpleasant ones. Like you did with Thomas, unlock the fire needed to thaw out our feelings of abandonment, or the shame of feeling unworthy of love.

Help us let go of hurt and disillusionment. Then give us your steady warmth, Gracious God, to reach out to the abandoned, withdrawn, hurt, the fragile Byrons of our lives. Bathe us in your warm affections of love, gentleness, and compassion. Amen.

Suggested Ritual

Light a candle. Warm your hands from its glow. Then alone or with your family, pause to recognize and give a name to what you are feeling right at that moment. Then simply imagine holding your feeling gently in your hands. Ask yourself if it is OK simply to be one with this feeling—but not changing, fixing, or analyzing it. As you sit there, see if the story behind the feeling begins to tell itself. If possible, speak and listen to another person, accepting, without judgment, whatever is said.

IV
Tending the Garden Patch
■ ■ ■

"Seeds of peace and justice cannot spring up anywhere except in the good soil of freedom, spontaneity and love."
                                        THOMAS MERTON

Focus

Tending our gardens, though often tedious, is essential for their growth. One difficult aspect of caring for our gardens, especially for the inexperienced, is pruning a bush. Where do we begin? How much must we cut back? Often, the only way we learn whether we are tending our garden properly is by the fruit it produces. When our family is more free, more spontaneous, and loving, we can be sure that the seeds of peace and justice that we have planted are growing to their full stature. Jesus reminds us of this same truth:

> "I am the true vine, and my Father is the vinegrower. He removes every branch in me that bears no fruit. Every branch that bears fruit he prunes to make it bear more fruit" (Jn 15:1–2).

Tending a strawberry patch, like pruning a rose bush, demands regular care. In order for the strawberry patch to expand and find places to grow, all weeds, even the prettier ones, must be uprooted carefully, lest we disturb the plants. In fact, the following four essays suggest that we not only must pull the weeds, we have to fertilize and mulch, as well as prune and cut. What can appear to be cruel, becomes the highest form of affirmation. If we want the strawberries to grow to their absolute fullness, we must give each plant room to grow, spread, and become itself.

The same is true for us, our families, and the Church. With an honesty that is rooted in prayer, we will grow as God directs. Though the work will often be tedious and demanding, the rewards will make all our work worth the effort.

Reflection

In tending the garden patch:

- How do we express our dream of unity?
- In what ways do we yearn for peace and justice?
- How do you provide a safe place in your patch: physically, emotionally, and spiritually?

Sprouting Seeds

*In spring we forget
that the winter seed
Had to die
To live.*

Telling the Story

Throwing her winter jacket onto the chair, Maggie came rushing into the house, exclaiming, "Grandma, it's spring. I can smell it. And besides, I saw the first crocus this morning and Mom said she heard a robin sing. Let's go out into the garden." It didn't seem to matter to Maggie that our side yard still had patches of snow. Neither was she concerned with getting her jeans damp and dirty from kneeling on the wet earth. It was spring, and everything was different. Her spirit knew she would soon be lying under the trees after school, watching the clouds through the branches with their small, new leaves, feeling the sun's warmth, and dreaming about the summer to come.

Maggie's enthusiasm was contagious. Her grandpa decided that it was time to take the storm window out of his office sash in favor of a screen, and her grandma found the courage to muddle through the basement, looking for yard furniture. Maggie's brother, Peter, also knew it was spring. His daddy was turning over the soil in the garden, and he wondered out loud when we would have tomatoes again.

- ■ Take a moment, do you remember your own seasons of excitement and growth?
- ■ How can you bring that excitement to today's events?

Discovering the Meaning

Spring, in the northeast, is a wonderfully hopeful time. After a winter of worrying whether the next morning would bring snow, ice, and treacherous driving, one can sense the earth's rebirth as dawn breaks earlier and supper's preparation begins before darkness falls.

People of every culture and religious tradition seem to sense this same thing, and celebrate it. In the Near East, on the first day of spring, families offer peace to one another and place wheat, lentils, or alfalfa seeds in a bowl. In order to remind everyone that it takes a lifetime to learn about ourselves and acknowledge our faults, they let the seeds germinate for a few days. Only then, in a special ceremony, do they throw the sprouted seeds into running water, symbolically letting go of all family quarrels, and beginning the spring with renewed hope.

A study I recently read clearly shows how badly we need healing rituals like this in our society. Half of the young people, aged five to nine, it asserts, acknowledge hitting another child at least once in the past twelve-month period. Other children, intimidated by the violence, withdraw, avoid quarrels, and pretend nothing happened, leaving them with low self-esteem and a feeling of uncertainty about their ability to be assertive.

In another article, adolescents were asked what they worried about most for their families. Three areas emerged: verbal arguments, their parents' heavy drinking, and not getting along with their brothers and sisters. These are weighty burdens for our children to carry. Because some of us respond to conflict aggressively, while others withdraw, we need to learn how to speak our minds, voice our feelings, and settle disagreements through conversation, collaboration, and consensus. Otherwise, the cycle of violence, which produces winners and losers in our society, will continue unabated, and the enthusiasm of children like Maggie will be lost.

- Is there much competitiveness in your family?
- What can you do about it?
- What can we do to channel our children's aggressiveness?

Acting

What are our family quarrels about? How do our families handle conflict, let go of old resentments, and admit new ones? How do we, as parents, ask forgiveness when we have overreacted, misjudged, or treated our children unfairly? Native Americans use a device called the *Talking Stick* to help them respond to these questions and speak about their feelings and worries honestly. The rule is that only the person holding the stick may speak. Everyone else must listen respectfully until they have possession of the stick. Conversations that begin with the *Talking Stick* are often very healing.

To this, we might also want to incorporate the water rite of reconciliation, which comes to us from the Near East. Choose some seeds that will germinate easily and quickly, and place them in a bowl of water on your kitchen table. After they have sprouted, gather your family together near a stream and toss the newly sprouted seeds into the running water, praying that everyone will be willing to let go and begin anew to live in peace.

Remembering

The Song of Solomon says it this way:

> My beloved speaks and says to me: / "Arise, my love, my fair one, / and come away; / for now the winter is past, / the rain is over and gone. / The flowers appear on the earth; / the time of singing has come, / and the voice of the turtledove / is heard in our land. / The fig tree puts forth its figs, / and the vines are in blossom; / they give forth fragrance. / Arise, my love, my fair one, / and come away" (Song 2:10–13).

The Song of Solomon is one of the most evocative, sensuous, and beautiful books in the Bible. Describing Yahweh's love for Israel like a bridegroom's love for his bride, the author echoes the language of the prophets Isaiah and Jeremiah. God does not simply love us. Like a new bridegroom, God is in love with us. Wouldn't it be wonderful to proclaim this beautiful Scripture to one another around our family table this spring as we seek to heal one another and begin again? Parents might also want to choose a time like this to share stories with their children about their own courtship and marriage with its ups and downs.

- Can you imagine God loving us like a bridegroom loves his bride?
- How can we help our children understand the profound images of gardens and weddings?

Praying

Healing God,

Winter is past. Flowers appear. Fig trees bloom. Vines give off a fragrance. Dawn breaks earlier. The song of the dove is heard in the land. Celebrate your spring in us, Sowing God. Turn over the soil of our lives. Sprinkle the earth of our being with your lavish love and nourish the seeds that have long been dormant and hidden from your light. Awaken us to the sound of your springtime.

Give us spring courage to speak our minds and voice our feelings as we try to resolve conflicts. In our life together, Healer God, may there be no winners or losers, no competition for your love which is enough for everyone. Spring is both a sowing and healing time. Give us a *talking stick* to help us speak, and a *listening heart* to hear the worries and concerns of others. Help us as a family to enter into forgiveness and healing, and begin anew to live in your springtime peace. Amen.

Suggested Rituals

As a family, engage in a water rite of reconciliation. Germinate seeds in a bowl. Throw sprouted seeds into some running water as you symbolically let go of family quarrels, resentments, and anger. Offer a sign of peace to one another.

A Safe Place

Under a bed or a tree
Inside a big closet or my soul
I wait for you, O God
And dream.

Telling the Story

Jay was the quietest of children. In fact, he was so introverted that I would often learn about things he disliked, like swimming lessons, two years after they happened! So I was delighted, many years ago, when he called for me as he came home from school.

"Mom, can we talk about something?"

Surprised by his request, I immediately put down the telephone, turned the gas lower on the stove, looked him right in the eye, and said: "Sure, Jay, what's on your mind?"

Without taking my eyes from his, my peripheral vision got larger and I couldn't help but see that his hair was getting very long. Making a mental note to ask his father to take him to the barber's that weekend, I also noticed that his pants were too short. Could he have grown that much in a month? Lost now, I tried to recover but was too late.

Jay said: "I'm sorry, Mom, you must have a lot on your mind. I'll come back later when you have more time."

While I had welcomed Jay into the physical space of our home, I wasn't really listening to him. Jay knew, instinctively, that this was not the time to tell his story. Even using the parent effectiveness skills I had learned, and thrilled that Jay was finally going to confide in me, I was distracted and unable to remain focused. By thinking about what was going to happen in the future, I was unable to stay in the present moment and lost an opportunity to listen to my very quiet son.

■ How do you feel when you are unable to listen to or hear others?

- Is there a faith response you can use to help you be a better listener?

Discovering the Meaning

Children have a profound emotional need for acceptance and affirmation. A person's tone of voice, the rolling of their eyes in exasperation, whispering behind someone's back, mocking laughter, and jeering smiles can all contribute to making little ones feel socially incompetent. Years ago, there was an IALAC (*I Am Lovable And Capable*) sign that we were invited to wear. Every time we experienced a "put down," or someone not listening to us, we were supposed to tear off a piece of the sign. You can imagine the size of Jay's sign when I was unable to put aside my own agenda and listen to him.

Children need our undivided attention to know they can feel emotionally safe with us, and also so that they need not be afraid to express their difficult feelings, or talk about ideas that are confusing to them. They also need to know that we will really listen to them before we formulate an answer. Not answering the telephone, as well as shutting off the television, radio, or computer is a good first step to show them that we are really listening.

- What do you need to shut off in order to be able to listen openly to others?
- How do you feel when others give you their undivided attention?

Acting

In our home, we have both a mesuzah and a Celtic blessing on the doorpost. These doorway prayers that welcome all into the safety of our home, originating from our Jewish and Irish heritages, remind us that God is present in all our comings and goings. Crossing the threshold, everyone is invited to let go of where they have been, and open themselves up to where they are now.

We encourage our children and grandchildren to touch the mesuzah and the Celtic blessing when they enter our home to give them the assurance that they are safe, and that they can ask difficult or troubling questions without fear. We don't want them to look at us simply as authority figures, anxious to impart our views and not really interested in what they are thinking or feeling. When children sense that we have a "message" rather than a real question, certain exciting conversations that might foster the life of the spirit among us cease. If children don't feel comfortable sharing their innermost thoughts with us or one another, religion becomes just an exercise in learning facts about God, the Church, and how to behave as Christians. Our religious imaginations shut down. In a setting like this, a profound appreciation of our religious tradition becomes impossible. No wonder our children sometimes don't want to talk about religion! And children like Jay turn away from us because we have so much on our minds!

More important, prayer becomes wooden and stiff. Our children feel "like they're in church," and they refuse to share their experiences and hopes. On the other hand, when children feel free to breathe, speak, and dream, religious celebrations become occasions of faith formation, and our families have a new vitality.

One way to assure our children that the environment is safe is to invite them to get involved early on in their lives. Listen closely to what they say. Assure them that they can express themselves freely. Your full attention also challenges them to pay close attention to whomever is speaking. With younger children, a quiet song and a gentle prayer can assure them that this is a time to listen, explore, and celebrate God's warm and safe love.

Sacred gestures can often convey the assurance of safety more powerfully than words. Lighting a candle reminds everyone that they are about to enter sacred space and time. When children begin to associate this gesture with emotional and spiritual safety, you will not have to say anything else. Lighting the candle will tell them that this is quiet time, a holy time when they can rest in the arms of God without fear.

Long ago, people had the perimeters of their property blessed for safety, and holly was hung in homes for protection. We may smile at these customs, but they reflect our need for both physical and emotional safety. The Church also recognizes this need by offering "sanctuary" to refugees and political exiles.

When our grandchildren join us for dinner, we invite them to ring bells to call everyone to the table. We "image" the ringing bells clearing a safe space, inviting all to share freely. The bells, like the mesuzah, help us remember that we are entering a sacred time and place.

We also begin group meetings with the ringing of a gentle gong, an invitation for everyone to become quiet and remember why we have gathered. By listening to and receiving this soft sound, we commit ourselves to respect whatever is heard and said.

Remembering

Jesus taught us this very same lesson when his disciples, who had their own agenda, were trying to keep the little children away from him:

> Then little children were being brought to him in order that he might lay his hands on them and pray. The disciples spoke sternly to those who brought them; but Jesus said, "Let the little children come to me, and do not stop them; for it is to such as these that the kingdom of heaven belongs." And he laid his hands on them and went on his way (Mt 19:13–15).

Hearing Jesus' invitation helped those children overcome their fear of not being accepted, and assured them that Jesus was preparing a safe place for them. In the ancient world, children learned early on that, as children, they were virtually without any value. They had no legal rights until they became adults. In fact, the Aramaic word for child also means servant or slave. Jesus, who came to us like a child, is also our servant. By calling children to himself, he challenges us not only to accept children as fully human, and worthy of all that is good, but also to become children and servants ourselves. In other words, Jesus' touch told the children that they were emotionally and spiritually safe with him. We do the same thing when we are at the doors of our homes, classrooms, and playgrounds to greet our children with love and acceptance.

- Is there anyone in your life who you think of as having less value than others?
- How can you make them feel safe, wanted, and cared for?
- At times, do you feel that you have little or no value and are neither needed nor appreciated?
- How can you respond to these feelings with faith?

Praying

God of All Safe Places,
Sometimes we're distracted, and sometimes unfocused. But our heart and ears yearn to be open to your presence in our lives through others. Help us to put our own agenda aside and listen to the subtle cries for acceptance and love from all the Jays in our life. Just as the touch of Jesus offered shelter to the children, God of All Safe Places, give us places that are safe—emotionally, physically, and spiritually—where we can tell our story, in our homes, classes, community, and "under a bed or a tree." Amen.

Suggested Ritual

Ring a bell and bless your doorways for safety.

> *Bless our comings and goings, our hellos*
>   *and good-byes,*
> *our letting go of where we have been,*
> *our openness to where we are now.*
> *May this threshold welcome all people*
>   *into a safe place.*

Fishing

*Our bodies, like earth itself,
know eternal truths
long before our minds.*

Telling the Story

Almost every Sunday morning after Mass when I was a boy, my Dad and I would take the long walk to the Hudson River. After crossing the railroad tracks, we would come to the pier and slowly walk from fisherman to fisherman to see what, if anything, they had caught. It was a gentle time and, for almost a year, I didn't realize that my Dad knew most of the people we passed.

One Sunday, shortly after I turned eight, my Dad began to introduce me to the crowd on the pier.

"This is Mr. Evans, Johnny," he said.

I stuck out my hand to Mr. Evans, who took it, smiled and said: "Hello, Johnny, do you like to fish?"

Fishing was one of the things I liked best. I nodded my head vigorously.

He asked, "Would you like to watch my line for a few minutes?"

"Sure," I said, almost too excited to speak.

Mr. Evans and my Dad walked away, caught up in conversation. My eyes never moved from the tip of his fishing rod. I so hoped a fish would bite that I reached for the pole almost every time a small wave moved the line, even just a little bit. Too soon, my Dad and Mr. Evans were back.

"No luck, Johnny?" Mr Evans asked.

"Not a thing," I said, trying to sound like the other men on the pier, never taking my eyes from the rod tip.

"Maybe next time," Mr. Evans said.

That was the signal for Dad and I to begin our walk home. Though disappointed that I hadn't caught a fish, just the opportunity to try was wonderful.

"Mr. Evans is a nice man, isn't he, Johnny," my Dad asked.
"Yesssss," I breathed.
Mr. Evans was black.

- Can you think of a lesson you learned as a child, on your own, without any instruction?
- Can you think of another that you still need to learn?

Discovering the Meaning

How can we introduce our children to people of other races, cultures, and religious traditions? My Dad's wisdom offers us some clues. Social scientists tell us that children do not naturally pay attention to race. They learn about it through their relationships with others, especially adults. Years ago, I learned this simple fact from the daughter of good friends. Suzie talked about Amanda all the time, but because she lived in "suburbia" and took the bus to school each day, I never met Amanda until I attended a school play. The fact that Amanda was black mattered not at all to Sue. Amanda was a friend with whom she explored and discovered life as a child. We, as adults, also need to find these same truths in our faith tradition and hold them up for reflection and prayer.

- Has racial prejudice ever affected you and your family?
- What did it feel like?
- What can we do about racial prejudice at home in order to make Jesus' dream of a world of unity come alive?

Acting

One simple way to promote racial understanding and acceptance is to celebrate the holidays and feast days that honor people of different races. January offers us the opportunity to gather with our families and parishes to remember the life and work of Martin Luther

King, Jr., who was so committed to understanding, reconciliation, nonviolence, and prayer. Probably more than any other American of the twentieth century, Martin Luther King, Jr., helped all Americans recognize the systemic racism so present in our national psyche, not by storming white communities or resorting to other forms of violence but by holding up a mirror into which all of us could look. That is why when he wrote, "I have a dream that my four little children will one day live in a nation where they will not be judged by the color of their skin, but the content of their character," we knew he was speaking the truth.

Reading the book of Exodus, which recounts the story of the Jewish people set free from slavery, can also help us launch good conversations. We might ask family members to name the person who sets them free to see and appreciate all people as children of God. We might also want to ask our children whether they have ever been the object of prejudice, and, if so, what it felt like. Offering one another opportunities for honesty about how badly we feel when we are excluded because of the way we look, talk, or believe frees us to understand what a terrible injustice it is to reject others because of the color of their skin or their national origin. If possible, it would also be wonderful to gather with one or two other families to celebrate Martin Luther King, Jr., day. Whenever possible, these gatherings ought to be interracial. Meeting people, and listening to their stories over a meal and a prayer, is always more powerful than just reading about racism in a book. I think Mr. Evans and my Dad would agree.

Remembering

Because of its strong and even frightening language, the beginning of the third chapter of Paul's letter to the church in Galatia is a good place to start:

> You foolish Galatians! Who has bewitched you? It was before your eyes that Jesus Christ was publicly exhibited as crucified! The only thing I want to learn from you is this:

Did you receive the Spirit by doing the works of the law or by believing what you heard? Are you so foolish? Having started with the Spirit, are you now ending with the flesh? Did you experience so much for nothing? (...) There is no longer Jew or Greek, there is no longer slave or free, there is no longer male and female; for all of you are one in Christ Jesus (Gal 3:1–4, 28).

When we are filled with fear, on the defensive, or have a desire for power over others, racism can be caught. In Paul's language, we can be stupid, and find ourselves naturally targeting those who appear to be different or "less" than we are. We allow ourselves to listen to comments that reinforce stereotypes about African Americans, Asians, and Latins, even going so far as telling racial or ethnic jokes. When children are taught to laugh at the way people look, talk, or carry themselves, they unconsciously learn to think of themselves as better and measure themselves with respect to others, rather than in the light of the Gospel. When parents experience prejudice hurting their children, their hearts break. There is no better time than the present to foster conversation and prayer in our homes about different races and cultures. When we quietly name our fears and hurts, we can teach our children, firsthand, how racism damages the body of Christ.

- What do you think of Paul's strong language when he addressed the Galatians?
- Could you ever imagine speaking so directly to others?
- If so, when, and under what circumstances?

Praying

God of All Dreams,
    Together, let us take the long walk to meet the fishing pier crowd of our lives: people of different races, cultures, and religious traditions; people who know what it feels like to be excluded and rejected

because of their skin color or national origin. Deepen our understanding of what it means to be brothers and sisters made in your image and likeness.

Give us hands and hearts to build a world where equality and justice, freedom, and peace will grow and flourish. Renew the dream of who we are and what we can be as your people. Confront us with the prejudice and racism of our lives and pledge us, God of All Colors, to loving, not hating; understanding, not anger; to making peace, not war.

Renew the dream of who we are and what we can be as your people. God of All Dreams, awaken us to your voice of compassion that calls us to work for peace and justice in our world so that, one day, we can join hands with you and say: "Free at last, free at last. Great God Almighty, in your love, we are free at last." Amen.

Suggested Ritual

Designate and light a "Dream Candle of Peace." Name and give thanks for the dream-makers and dream-keepers of our lives.

Diversity

Though every snowflake is unique
We sometimes forget
They are really more alike
Than different.

Telling the Story

Gerry and Marla are from the "old school." Educated at community colleges, they married when they were both twenty-two and started a family almost immediately. Gerry is an accountant for a small construction firm, and Marla has served on the school board several times. Their oldest child, Maria, is an artist. Gentle, creative, and very extroverted, Maria has no intention of settling down before she turns thirty. Her sister, Jeanne, on the other hand, opened her own business when she was twenty-one and wants to retire by the time she is forty. While there is little visible tension between the sisters, they rarely socialize with each other.

This family, so diverse in goals and temperament, offers us a glimpse into the twenty-first century. Either we learn to live well with diversity, or we will collapse. The same is true, we think, for the Church. Population projections tell us that the majority of American Catholics will be of Hispanic origin by early in this century. Another significant minority will be the Asian community. How we live with our increasing diversity in both the home church as well as the world church will be one of the most important tests of our enduring religious presence in this country.

I had a graphic example of this while I was on a pilgrimage in the Holy Land. One church I visited had the Our Father printed on its walls in dozens of languages. Hearing this beautiful prayer spoken in many different tongues at the Eucharist both startled and thrilled me. It brought me to the realization that we are so alike in creed, yet so different in how we express our beliefs. No doubt, diversity can be baffling, even overwhelming at times, but as long as we guard against defining ourselves as being better than people who look or sound different from us, we will grow in faith. More important, standing in the shoes of the people of other cultures in order to have firsthand proof of our similarities, will be the groundwork that allows us to name and accept our differences.

- How do you handle diversity in your own life?

- Have you had any good intercultural or interracial experiences? What were they like?

Acting

Experts often remind us that parenting will be much more complex and difficult in the twenty-first century. Children are put into daycare programs earlier and earlier, where they must learn complex socialization skills much sooner than generations before them. Becoming aware of differences among themselves, not the least of which are race, culture, and religion, is a great challenge. If we hope to empower our children to create a world that is free of racism and religious intolerance, then we need to keep growing in our knowledge and appreciation of our own faith, as well as the religious traditions of people all over the world.

We can also help our children immensely by modeling accepting behavior in our own homes. Not judging, criticizing, advising, lecturing, or moralizing, but affirming and celebrating one another's strengths will help our children learn how to live well together.

Consider trying the following exercise as an introduction to accepting the diversity in your own home. On any given day, place the following words on your refrigerator: *Great, Good, OK, Yuck,* and *Let's start over*. Encourage family members to place their names under the word or phrase that best describes how they feel that day. Then at supper, invite each person to express the reason(s) for their choice. We usually begin with those family members who have had either "Good" or "Great" days. Those who put their names under "Let's start over" usually need more time before they can open up to the group. When the meal is completed, ask each person to place their hands on the shoulder of the person nearest them and say: "Regardless of how you feel, I accept you today just as you are."

Remembering

We have only to read the fifteenth chapter of the Acts of the Apostles to know how Peter and Paul struggled with the diversity of Christianity as it expanded beyond Jerusalem:

> After there had been much debate, Peter stood up and said to them, "My brothers, you know that in the early days God made a choice among you, that I should be the one through whom the Gentiles would hear the message of the good news and become believers. And God, who knows the human heart, testified to them by giving them the Holy Spirit, just as he did to us; and in cleansing their hearts by faith he has made no distinction between them and us. Now therefore why are you putting God to the test by placing on the neck of the disciples a yoke that neither our ancestors nor we have been able to bear?" (Acts 15:7–10).

While the Acts of the Apostles reminds us that the early Church struggled mightily with how Jews and Gentiles might live well together as a community of faith centered in Jesus, it also challenges us to find our way through contemporary conflicts that are rooted in race, religion, culture, and gender. The issue of diversity has not only not gone away, it appears to be a far more important concern as we fully embrace the twenty-first century. Television has made it almost impossible for people to be ignorant of other nations and cultures. Famines, wars, and natural disasters of every kind are almost immediately broadcast on our television sets, demanding our attention and compassion. Our computers and fax machines, moreover, allow us almost instant conversation with people in other countries and cultures, covering subjects as simple as the Olympics and as important as war and hunger. Our ability to use technology creatively may very well make or break our efforts not only at evangelization but also at human living as well.

- What do you think about Peter's challenge to the early Christian community not to unduly burden new converts with unnecessary rules?
- How successful are we, in our families and neighborhoods, at applying the same suggestion?

Praying

God of Diversity,

We are the work of your hands. You create each of us alike, yet different; unique, yet the same. Your hands, Creator God, continue to touch, mold, and shape us into one people, interdependent, your family of diversity.

"Multiculturalize" our lives. Let us be witnesses to the power and possibility of diversity in our world through the way we live and respect people who are of different temperaments, nations, races, religions, or genders than our own. Let us marvel at the extroversion of a Maria, the business-minded actions of a Jeanne, the school board interests of a Marla. With Peter and Paul, in the Acts of Apostles, continue to challenge us in our struggle with the diversity of being a Christian.

Deepen our appreciation of people who look and sound different than we do. Help us to stand in the shoes of others as we name and accept our differences. Rid us of the "us against them" way of thinking. Restore all things to you, God of Oneness and Diversity.

Most Holy and Boundless Breath of Creation, forever and ever, we bow to you. Your Holy Spirit belongs to everyone. Amen.

Suggested Ritual

Sit and repeat the holy sound of a blessing of wholeness to others, in different languages: *Shanti, Shalom, Salaam, Peace.* Then add your own.

V

Growing Garden Plants
■ ■ ■

> *"As long as the earth endures,*
> *seedtime and harvest, cold and heat,*
> *summer and winter, day and night,*
> *shall not cease."*
>
> Genesis 8:22

Focus

Growth is such a mysterious process! Think, for a moment, about a child you have not seen for several months. How different he or she can appear in just a few weeks! While it may not appear to be as startling, spiritual growth is just as remarkable. A young person makes a retreat and returns changed, at least for a few weeks or months. Afterwards, though the growth might not be as rapid, the effects are lasting. Faith has taken root in their hearts, and it will not be easily uprooted. The following four essays remind us, like the strawberry runner that seeks new growth, that even though it may remain below the earth for a long time, faith is there, growing, deepening, and getting ready to help each of us find a new and more constant way of being alive in the spirit.

It is good to pay attention to these subtle rhythms of our faith growth, not to control them, but to be drawn into the holy mystery that grounds them. God is everywhere, we soon discover, not as an abstract truth or belief but as a dynamic energy in whom all things live, move, and have their being.

The paradox of faith growth is summed up for Christians when Jesus says, "Very truly, I tell you, unless a grain of wheat falls into the earth and dies, it remains just a single grain; but if it dies, it bears much fruit" (Jn 12:24). Growth comes only through death. The Gospel, internalized as a living way of life, transforms not only our individual behavior but our communities as well. When we are ready to die to self-absorption, greed, and self-reliance, the Gospel can finally do its work.

Reflections

By being present to growing garden plants

- How do we see sickness, loss, failure, mistakes, death, and dying?
- What are our family rituals for change?
- What is the rhythm of our family year?
- How do we provide for growth and still remain centered?

Helping Children Manage Loss

Dad's death
seems unreal,
like wrinkles
hidden by
early morning shadows.
Until noon.

Telling the Story

Miriam's dad had been sick for many years when she finally placed him in a nursing home. Though painful for both her and her family, she could no longer ignore his progressive decline due to Alzheimer's disease. Like so many other sufferers, Miriam's father often forgot where and who he was. Neither could he remember his phone number nor those of his children. More painful still was the fact that, although he would always be polite to visitors, especially his children, he would startle them just a few minutes into the conversation by asking them to tell him their names. That is why I was so surprised at his greeting when I visited him a few weeks ago. Upon seeing me, he said: "Hello, Gaynell, it's good to see you. Sit down, please."

Henry's politeness was typical for him. Always the gentleman, he tried to stand when I entered the room, and immediately reached to turn off the television. Surprised that he recognized me, I began to talk about the weather and the nursing home with him. He was happy, he told me, and glad for the care he was receiving. The mask fell away, however, when I asked him how he liked the food (he had been a gourmet cook in his younger years). He looked at me blankly for a moment, then responded: "I'm not really sure, I haven't had a meal yet." By that time, Henry had been in the nursing home for almost a month. Fooled for a moment by his ability to remember my name, I could no longer deny the effects this disease had on him. Near tears, I began to remind him of the wonderful meals he had prepared for all of us at his daughter's home, but, by then, he had already fallen asleep.

- How do you imagine yourself caring for the elderly, especially your parents?

- How can we walk with others whose parents are sick and appear distant because of their illness?

Discovering the Meaning

Illness and aging, somewhat inevitable events in all our lives, are especially difficult on the children. For more than twenty-five years, I have had the privilege of inviting children to pray about the sickness and deaths of their grandparents and relatives. These sessions are always moving for me, as well as the children. They are also especially easy to do since the children are naturally drawn to quiet and reverence when they have to face, and pray about, the sickness and deaths of their relatives.

Chad, a precocious nine-year-old, reminded me of the special relationship children can have with grandparents when he stayed after class one day to tell me that he wanted to speak his Grandpa's name at the prayer service, but couldn't, because it hurt too much. Tears streaming down his face, he told me his Grandpa was his best friend. Crying with him, I reminded Chad that Jesus cried when his best friend Lazarus died. I also suggested to him that Jesus probably cried a great deal when his friends were either hurt or rejected. Chad agreed and told me that he had asked Jesus to take good care of his Grandpa.

When a disease like Alzheimer's attacks a family member, it can be doubly difficult. Even though they are still alive, our relatives "feel" dead to us. Unable to either respond to or understand our frustration, they often slowly stop speaking altogether. When this happens, we need to help those people, and especially our children, manage their loss and develop coping skills.

- What do you think is the best way to share death and dying with children?

- Can you think of a way to explain a disease, like Alzheimer's, to a child?

Acting

Holidays, birthdays, and anniversaries can be an especially fitting time to help our families face the profound sense of loss we all feel when either a family member or friend is seriously ill or dies. Sometimes, we ask family members to draw a picture of what they shared with that person, or even to write a letter to that person saying how much they love and miss him or her. Sometimes, people bring items that belonged to the person: jewelry, a cap, a dish, a sweater, a rosary, or some perfume and place the item in the middle of the kitchen table. After we gather for supper and light a candle, everyone is encouraged to speak briefly about the item they brought, what that person meant to them, or one quality the person had that they want to live on in their own lives.

After supper, those people who either wrote a letter or made a drawing are invited to share their creations. This simple exercise helps us remember to appreciate each day we are given and to be grateful for the rich times we have spent together. It also reminds us to put aside the small differences we might have experienced with one another so that our family can really be united.

Remembering

In the Gospel according to Luke, Jesus demonstrates tremendous compassion for a widow:

> Soon afterwards he went to a town called Nain, and his disciples and a large crowd went with him. As he approached the gate of the town, a man who had died was being carried out. He was his mother's only son, and she was a widow;

and with her was a large crowd from the town. When the Lord saw her, he had compassion for her and said to her, "Do not weep." Then he came forward and touched the bier, and the bearers stood still. And he said, "Young man, I say to you, rise!" The dead man sat up and began to speak, and Jesus gave him to his mother. Fear seized all of them; and they glorified God, saying, "A great prophet has risen among us!" and "God has looked favorably on his people!" (Lk 7:11–16).

In the ancient world, women had virtually no rights. They could not inherit their husband's property and were dependent upon their sons to provide for them. The widow in this passage has only one son, and without him, she would be at the mercy of the community. While the miracle of raising the young man from the dead is great, perhaps it is an even more profound show of his love that Jesus does not want the widow left alone. In returning her son to her, Jesus gives the widow, and us, a new lease on life.

- How do we help our families face the reality of sickness and death?

- Do we have any family rituals that can help us face difficult times?

Praying

God of Compassion,
Like Miriam's Dad, I sometimes forget where and who I am in your life, God. I simply look at you, blankly, and then you help me to remember your name, and your presence in me. Often, I hide in the early morning shadows. Noon comes, and even though it is still unreal, and difficult to accept, I face diminishment and dying within myself and others.

God, you have visited us. You cry and weep with us. As Jesus was moved, out of pity, for the widow whose only son had died, come forward and, with your touch, let life awaken inside us again. Stir your compassion for all of life into my heart. When asked by a friend how she prayed for another person, the mystic Julian of Norwich said: "I look at you, I look at God and I keep on looking at God." Like Julian, give me your eyes of compassion and pray for all of life.

Pray in me, God of Compassion, for other people. Help me to look and gaze with you in love and care for others as well as myself. I place my hand on my eyes, asking for the gift to see, on my heart to be open to the suffering of others. Take my hand in yours. Together with others, let us take a compassionate walk through life. Amen.

Suggested Ritual

Sit in silence. Pray for openness.

Ask God: For whom would you have me pray? Allow the face or name of someone to come forth.

Ask God: What is your prayer in me for this person? Listen.

Ask God: What would you like me to do or be on their behalf? Open your heart and receive the answers.

Honesty About Our Failures

*Is it still a Eucharist
when eating alone,
a prisoner in my own home,
I yearn
for my family?*

Telling the Story

Kara was troubled. No one was home again for supper. Somewhat distracted, she took a burrito from the freezer, put it in the microwave oven, and waited for her instant supper to emerge. Another meal alone, she thought, not my vision of family life, and not what I say to the other religious-education teachers!

Just last week, Karen had engaged in a long and animated discussion with two third-grade teachers about the importance of family meals. While they agreed, they told her they often felt overwhelmed by the number of activities they had to attend. Soccer practice, ballet lessons, and visits to parents and grandparents all took up an enormous amount of time. More important, they both also held part-time jobs to help supplement their husbands' incomes. And they were the fortunate ones! Most of their friends worked full time to help meet their considerable family expenses. Meals together were few and far between, and then when they did take place, they were often interrupted by phone calls and other annoying distractions.

Kara had insisted. Without family meals together, it was impossible to either understand or appreciate the power of the Eucharist. She believed in what she was saying. Now this. Eating alone, she flicked on the television for company and wondered, half aloud, what she could or should do about her family life and the lack of time they spent together. She also worried about what her children were subconsciously learning about family life when they had so many activities and events to attend.

- What do you do when you feel alone?
- Do you talk with others about the stress of family life?

Discovering the Meaning

In recent years, theologians have been asserting that authentic theological reflection begins with an honest and open description of the reality in which we find ourselves. Families, households, or domestic churches need to learn the same lesson.

Children know this intuitively. Not long ago, I attended a baptismal party at which a seven-year-old burst into the kitchen where a number of us were talking and blurted out: "Grandpa is drunk again." Despite her mother's embarrassment that little girl was offering her family a powerful opportunity to face the unhealthy reality of their family life, and to do something about it.

While the party may not have been either the time or the place to begin, I prayed that my friend would find a way to put aside her shame and take the first step in facing the reality of her family life. She needed to find a time and a place to talk about her father's drinking. Even though we might not be faced with the very same kind of humiliation my friend felt, we still need to heed the warning signs we receive about family stress, and make an effort to put aside time to talk regularly with one another about how well or poorly we are living our family values. The Book of Common Prayer puts it this way: "Help them to take failure, not as a measure of their worth, but as a chance for a new start."

- What do you think about the notion of the domestic church?
- Is your domestic church a safe place where illnesses like alcoholism and other substance abuses can be faced?

Acting

Sometimes, we avoid facing failure and even go so far as to deny it, stating: "This can't be happening to me," or "What have I done to deserve this?" At other times, our frustration explodes, and we say something like: "It's just not fair." That is why we need to gather regularly as families. If your family finds it difficult to face up to its failures, try this activity. Light a candle and ask: "What rests heavy inside of you right now?" Let the question sink it. After a little while, ask your family members to visualize and share their failures with one another by giving them names and colors. Families who are willing to take this vulnerable step are often richly rewarded for their efforts.

You might also ask your family members to choose an image or symbol that honestly describes how they see themselves and then draw it. One person might say: "I'm an empty table. No one sits with me to talk." Or another, "I am a clock with its hands running out of control. I have too many activities, and not enough time nor the ability to finish what I start." After everyone has had a opportunity to share, pray simply out of gratitude for their honesty and the feelings expressed.

Remembering

The Gospel also teaches us this lesson very clearly. In the fourth chapter of John's Gospel, Jesus has a long conversation with a Samaritan woman. Now, since Samaritans rejected the religious authority of Jerusalem, its residents were despised. By talking with the Samaritan woman, Jesus risked scandal and ritual impurity. Nevertheless, apparently touched by the woman's honesty and boldness, Jesus promises that if she drinks the "water of salvation," she will never again be thirsty. Impressed when the woman has the courage to ask for water, Jesus tells her to call her husband and come back. The woman responds:

> "I have no husband." Jesus said to her, "You are right in saying, 'I have no husband'; for you have had five husbands, and the one you have now is not your husband. What you have said is true!" (...) Then the woman left her water jar and went back to the city. She said to the people, "Come and

see a man who told me everything I have ever done!..." (Jn 4:17–18,28–29).

Jesus' insight and honesty helped her to face her life and begin to change. In the same way, when we attempt to gather in faith as families, and honestly face our failures, we offer a wonderful sign to other families, as well as our parishes, that we understand the importance of being Christ's followers at home.

- Are we able to reach beyond differences in our families and neighborhoods?
- Do we have the courage to face both our needs as well as our failures honestly?
- How can we give witness to our faith at home?

Praying

God of All Honesty,
Another instant supper. Alone. Where do I turn for company? TV? A book? Everyone is busy. Meals bond a family together, and deepen friendships. Where is everyone? Having fewer meals with my family brings me pain, deep inside. I wonder, do you feel the same way, Nourishing God, when my meals and presence with you lessen?

How do I become more honest about my failures, and not run away from them? Like the Samaritan woman, I welcome you, Jesus, to tell me "everything I have ever done." Be honest. Help me face myself, my failures, and begin to change. Let me be bold and honest in conversation. Amen.

Suggested Ritual

Spend a few moments becoming aware of your breathing. Get in touch with one thing with which you are not at peace—perhaps where you have failed. Breathe that failure into the space where the God of All Honesty and Compassion lives, deep inside. Then, through your breathing in and out, connect with other people in the world who are struggling with the same failures. Your pain is theirs, and their pain becomes yours. Be one in compassion and honesty with all that is.

Learning Patience

Stumbling up and down steps
I wonder
whether my feet
are really made for walking.
Only God seems not to care.

Telling the Story

Tim, nine years old and precocious, was stirring a cookie mix. When he added a third egg to the batter, I had to stop myself from interrupting. I wanted him to recognize his mistake, but I also wanted him to be successful in baking cookies. As I almost literally held my tongue, Tim turned to me and said: "Don't worry Uncle Jack, an extra egg makes the cookies fluffier, and that's the way I like them."

I smiled to myself, and assured Tim that I was behind him the whole way, but my spirit started to reflect upon my usual manner of helping others. It is very difficult for me to step back and allow others, especially children, to make mistakes. I want them to get things right the first time, and every time after that. Even though I had good intentions, my method often undermines the children's confidence in themselves. When I jump in too quickly to help, I am reminded of my own childhood, and how my mother had raised us. A perfectionist, my mother preferred to do everything herself and often lost patience with us. I knew she wanted us to experience success, but her methods made me very reluctant to try new projects. The phrase, "What will Mom think?" was never far from my mind.

Even though we may not realize it, our children want to please us; they want to live in a way that will make us proud of their accomplishments. When we rush in to correct, rebuke, direct, or control them, they are naturally tempted to stop trying. Wary of finding us looking over their shoulders, they even pretend not to care, or worse, decide to live in a way that directly rejects our authority and role. Our willingness, like Pope John XXIII said, "to see everything, overlook a great deal, and correct a little" will give our children the confidence they need to think well of themselves and work alongside us.

- Can you remember a time when an adult couldn't stop helping you?
- What did it feel like?

Discovering the Meaning

A few years ago, I went on a long trip. While I was gone, one of the friars with whom I lived, thinking that he was being very helpful, went into my office and straightened out my desk. When I returned, it was all I could do not to scream. Though I am not the neatest person in the world, I had things arranged on my desk in a way that made sense to me. Even though he had the best of intentions, the friar who tried to help left me completely disoriented. I imagine he was waiting for a "thank you" of some kind from me, but I had everything I could do not to lose my temper!

Conversely, last week, I watched a young mother prepare supper with her five-year-old daughter, Amy. It was an event worthy of God! After mom had carefully washed, peeled, and cut up the potatoes, talking all the while with Amy, she invited her daughter to put the potatoes into a big pot. Amy was very diligent and needed no help, even when she missed the pot. She got off her chair, picked up the potato, washed it, and put it into the pot. Amy's mom seemed perfectly at peace during all of this, and I wanted to put her on video. In a few short minutes, Amy was off to another project, but I had learned another lesson. When parents are patient and inclusive with their children, their children are patient in return with them!

- What are some signs that indicate our children are capable of taking on new tasks and challenges?
- How can we allow them to express their independent selves?

Acting

Virginia Satir, in *Peoplemaking*, said: "Communication is the greatest single factor affecting a person's health and relationship with others." If we want to be effective communicators, we need to ask our children how much help they need, and not presume we know what is best for them all of the time. Engaging children in conversation about how we might help them will take extra time, but their realization that we trust them to make good decisions will build their confidence and trust in us. If we expect children to learn the importance of patience, listening, and accompanying one another in faith, we need to find the time to let them make their own mistakes without always trying to fix things for them.

Take time, also, to tell your children about times in your life when someone helped you. How did you ask for help? How did they help? Get in touch with the way you help others. Do you rescue, protect, and give advice, or do you just take charge, even before you are asked? Or do you listen, affirm, and say things like: "I know you can do this"? Imagine opening one hand to your child saying, "What do you need right now?" Then, imagine opening your other hand to your child saying, "How can I help you?"

Remembering

In John's Gospel, after Jesus tells his friends that he will have to die to save them, there is a poignant phrase: "After Jesus had said this, he departed and hid from them" (Jn 12:36). We think we need to hide ourselves more from our children. Getting out of the way so they can learn about themselves, their skills, and the life of the spirit that dwells in them not only fosters their growth but ours as well. The following is just one of the many examples that Jesus himself gives us of this:

> There were two blind men sitting by the roadside. When they heard that Jesus was passing by, they shouted, "Lord, have mercy on us, Son of David!" The crowd sternly ordered them

to be quiet; but they shouted even more loudly, "Have mercy on us, Lord, Son of David!" Jesus stood still and called them, saying, "What do you want me to do for you?" They said to him, "Lord, let our eyes be opened." Moved with compassion, Jesus touched their eyes. Immediately they regained their sight and followed him (Mt 20:30–34).

Isn't it fascinating to listen to Jesus ask the blind men what they want? At first, Jesus' question seems unnecessary, even silly. But when we realize that he is allowing the persons in need to choose how they want to live, we realize just how sensitive his question really is. And, we learn that he is teaching us an important lesson. We must admit to ourselves and also tell the Lord what we need. Otherwise, we are asking God to read our minds.

- Do we really know what we need for our faith journey?
- Once we do recognize our needs, are we willing to ask God for help?

Praying

God of Patience,

I, too, am along the side of the road, unable to see, crying out for help, and I hear your voice: *"What do you want me to do?"* Well, don't you know? Isn't it evident? But, Jesus, always the Patient One, you wait, honoring, and respecting me to name and acknowledge my needs. You do not just rush in. You trust me, like the blind ones, to come to my insight, to see and name my own wants and, like you, to be present with others as they do the same.

Like the determined hare, running frantically to the finish line, I sometimes rush compulsively into the lives of others—trying to protect, take charge, rescue, and fix things, giving advice, even when I am not asked for it. I do not trust in the fact that I am simply supposed to be there as another person discovers and develops skills for living life. Open my heart to the patience of the tortoise. Bring insight to my clouded eyes and, like the blind ones, let me follow you, walking slowly and patiently, together with all of life. Amen.

Suggested Ritual

Sit quietly with your eyes closed. Hear Jesus ask you: What do you want me to do? Answer him.

Then, let the face of someone you care about come into your mind. Hear yourself ask, as you open your hands on your lap: What do you want me to do? Hear that person's answer.

Extend your hands as you ask: How can I help you? Promise yourself to wait patiently for an answer.

Our Household Church

Ridicule,
like a sharp, stinging rain
hurts
before it cleanses.

Telling the Story

A friend with young teenagers and a toddler, laughing so she wouldn't cry, told me about a simple ritual she tried in her home when her husband was on a business trip. Even though her teenagers insisted the ritual was "stupid," and that the "food was getting cold," she plowed ahead, despite objections. While she managed to finish the ritual, her heart told her she didn't want to keep trying new prayer forms in her home. Her husband was away, her parents were struggling with health problems, and she was trying, unsuccessfully, to cope with the terrors of middle age. Were it not for her youngest child, whom she so wanted to know God at home, rituals would have been too much for her to manage.

I knew her feelings only too well! Almost every time Jack and I give a workshop about rituals for homes, we warn the participants that we share only those rituals that work, and don't tell them about the thousands that fail. Everyone laughs. They know that celebrating rituals at home is risky. There always seems to be at least one uncomfortable person in every group whose discomfort expresses itself in loud sighs, a constantly shifting chair, and protestations about everything and anything. Sometimes, the person who is most uncomfortable is an adult, even a spouse.

- How do you respond to the discomfort of a family member when you try to pray?
- What is it that sustains you along this journey?

Discovering the Meaning

Because most people in North America still seem to prefer that their religion and religious rituals be celebrated in church on Sunday mornings, we can sometimes mistakenly allow the institutional Church to provide for all our religious needs. When we do this, we abandon both our Jewish and early Christian roots. Religion in the early Church was a family affair, a celebration of the "household church," replete with home rituals. Our Jewish sisters and brothers still celebrate most of their important religious rituals at home. Sabbath, Seder meals for Passover, and building "tabernacles" for the feast of Succoth are only a few obvious examples.

If we really hope to reclaim the church of the home, and want our children to know the transforming power of family rituals, we need to remember our common heritage. Despite some family member's anxiety and resistance, we need to take more responsibility for faith formation in our homes. The faith that makes us willing to move gently forward, despite others' opposition, will be a wonderful lesson in integrity for our children and family members alike.

- What is it that most prevents us from creating and celebrating family prayer rituals at home?
- How can we support one another to pray as a family at home?

Acting

Authentic home rituals help families focus on their most important needs and concerns and express, through sacred gestures, what can never be adequately expressed in words. If, for instance, we decide to plant a tree to honor a family member who dies, the actual planting of the tree can help us symbolically to let go. When we also include some soil from that person's grave to nourish the new tree, we take yet a further step in accepting the unexpected death of someone who was dear to us. If, moreover, we visit and water the tree regularly, our attention to its new life deepens our commitment to living fully, while continuing to honor the person who has died.

A few months ago, when my husband Jim was preparing for cataract surgery, we felt the need for a simple ritual. Because Jim has always been a voracious reader, he was especially nervous about eye surgery. So were we. To calm ourselves a bit, we first chose to join hands and talk about our love for Jim. Then, in silence, we all laid our hands on Jim, and prayed that God would guide the surgeon's hands and help Jim to see well again. By naming our concerns, and extending our hands in blessing, we not only let Jim know of our love, we also called upon our faith to guide and sustain us. It was a touching moment and it brought everyone a certain degree of peace.

When we celebrate like this in our home, even the smallest children are invited to help us pray, and this is as it should be. We need to find ways to invite everyone, no matter how young or old, to have a role in our ritual prayers. When we prayed and blessed Jim, our grandchildren called the family to our home table of the Lord by ringing bells, just like they do every Sunday. They also reminded us, by their solemn manner, that everyone needed to be quiet for a few moments as we gathered. Only when they rang the bells a second time did people join hands and pray about their concerns and hopes for Jim.

As well, we light candles for most of the meals we share together. This can be an important rite of passage for children when they are recognized as being "old enough" to strike the match and light the candles. You might also want to consider the occasional "procession" from your living room to the dining area. Everyone, especially the children, love a parade. It signals the start of something important and different: our Sunday meal together.

Last week, in our religious-education program, a small miracle happened. As parents, children, and teachers gathered in our parish church for the presentation of some plays the children had prepared, everyone became really quiet. The parents appeared amazed. After thanking the children for paying such careful attention to one another, I invited all their teachers to come forward for a blessing. Hesitant at first, they slowly made their way to the front of the church. After everyone had gathered, I invited the children to stand and extend their hands over their teachers in a blessing. The children seemed to sense that this was a special moment. In a wonderful gesture of love and caring, they stretched their hands over their teachers and prayed: "O God, bless our teachers. Let them know how grateful we are for their patience and love of us. And let them feel your blessing of love with every step they take. Amen." There wasn't a dry eye in the church!

Remembering

The Scriptures are full of examples of people who refuse to quit, even in the face of overwhelming odds. Paul talks about "running the good race," and Jesus never turns his face from Jerusalem, no matter how difficult the path. Everyone knows the story of the centurion who comes to Jesus, asking for a cure for his serving boy even though he is not a Jew. And who can forget Zacchaeus climbing a tree to see Jesus despite the ridicule he must have received from the crowds? Listen to how this unfolds:

> A man was there named Zacchaeus; he was a chief tax collector and was rich. He was trying to see who Jesus was, but on account of the crowd he could not, because he was short in stature. So he ran ahead and climbed a sycamore tree to see him, because he was going to pass that way. When Jesus came to the place, he looked up and said to him, "Zacchaeus, hurry and come down; for I must stay at your house today." So he hurried down and was happy to welcome him. All who saw it began to grumble and said, "He has gone to be the guest of one who is a sinner." Zacchaeus stood there and said to the Lord, "Look, half of my possessions, Lord, I will give to the poor; and if I have defrauded anyone of anything, I will pay back four times as much." Then Jesus said to him, "Today salvation has come to this house…" (Lk 19:2–9).

Tax collectors were despised in Jesus' time. Not only did they collect taxes for the Roman invaders, they often overcharged those who knew no better. Observant Jews considered tax collectors unclean, making it impossible to share a meal with them. When Jesus confronts this practice and the attitudes of religious people in dismissing those they judge to be sinners, he challenges us all to reexamine our willing eagerness to judge others without knowing their full story.

The practice of faith is not easy, especially in our homes. Nevertheless, Jesus insists that our "Yes" mean "Yes," and our "No" mean "No." Fidelity to God's plan is the final measurement of our commitment to the Gospel.

- Who are the "tax collectors" in our families and societies?

- How do we look at, and treat them?

Praying

God of All Households,
A roof, walls, windows, doors, and floors—a refuge and place called home—and wonder of all wonders, you are there, God! And we do try, yet so often fail, to celebrate your presence as we express our needs and concerns through gestures and rituals. We are a home church! Extraordinary!

As you did with Zacchaeus, stay at our house as we plant a tree, light candles, ring bells, offer blessings, and listen to a story. Laugh with us, as our rituals sometimes evoke discomfort and loud sighs when what is intended is not realized. God of All Households, help us overcome our fear and reluctance to try new prayer forms in your church, our home. Amen.

Suggested Ritual

Light two candles—dedicating one to the past, naming people in our life who love us; and one to the future, as a symbol of hope for children everywhere. Then, holding hands in the present, name a need, concern, or cause for gratitude. If little ones are present, have them ring a bell(s) as a sign to call for silence to begin this ritual.

About the Authors
■■■

Rev. Jack Rathschmidt, a Capuchin Franciscan Friar, is the chaplain at the College of New Rochelle. Writer, teacher, and spiritual director, he is vitally interested in empowering lay people in the church. His e-mail address is jackratch@juno.com.

Gaynell Cronin, a DRE and pastoral associate for more than thirty years, has written dozens of film strips and videos for religious education, as well as ten books, among them the award-winning *Friend Jesus*. Wife, mother of four, and grandmother of eight, she is passionate about faith formation for families as home churches. Her e-mail address is gaynellcronin@juno.com.

Together they are columnists for *FaithWorks*, a monthly catechetical newsletter, and conduct retreats, parish mission and workshops on spirituality and home ritual. They have also written more than fifty videos for faith formation as well as the books, *Rituals for Home and Parish: Healing and Celebrating our Families* and *The Blessing Candles: 58 Simple Mealtime Prayers*.